John Miller was born in Coventry and was educated at the Perse School and Jesus College, Cambridge, before becoming a research fellow at Gonville and Caius College. He has been Professor of History at Queen Mary University of London (formerly Queen Mary College) since 1989. He is also a member of the council of the Huguenot Society of Great Britain and Ireland and has served on the Council of the Royal Historical Society, of which he has been a Fellow since 1978.

Titles available in the *Brief History* series

A BRIEF HISTORY OF

THE ENGLISH CIVIL WARS

Roundheads, Cavaliers and the
Execution of the King

JOHN MILLER

ROBINSON

Constable & Robinson Ltd
3 The Lanchesters
162 Fulham Palace Road
London W6 9ER
www.constablerobinson.com

First published in the UK by Robinson,
an imprint of Constable & Robinson Ltd, 2009

A copy of the British Library Cataloguing in Publication
Data is available from the British Library

ISBN: 978-1-84529-683-4

Printed and bound in the EU

1 3 5 7 9 10 8 6 4 2

CONTENTS

ABBREVIATIONS

Clarendon	E. Hyde, earl of Clarendon, *History of the Rebellion*, ed. W.D. Macray, 6 vols, Oxford, 1888
Gardiner, *Documents*	S.R. Gardiner (ed.), *Constitutional Documents of the Puritan Revolution, 1625–60*, 3rd edn, Oxford, 1951
Gardiner, *GCW*	S.R. Gardiner, *History of the Great Civil War, 1642–9*, 4 vols, London, 1893
Gardiner, *History*	S.R. Gardiner, *History of England, 1603–42*, 10 vols, London, 1883
HJ	*Historical Journal*
Kenyon	J.P. Kenyon, *The Stuart Constitution*, 2nd edn, Cambridge, 1986
Lindley	K. Lindley, *The English Civil War and Revolution: A Sourcebook*, London, 1998
Mendle	M. Mendle (ed.), *The Putney Debates of 1647*, Cambridge, 2001
Morrill, *Reactions*	J.S. Morrill (ed.), *Reactions to the English Civil War*, London, 1982

Morrill, *Revolt (1)*	J.S. Morrill, *The Revolt of the Provinces, 1630–50*, London, 1976
Morrill, *Revolt (2)*	J.S. Morrill, *Revolt in the Provinces 1630–48: The People of England and the Tragedies of War*, London, 1999 (This edition does not include the selection of documents in the 1976 edition)
P & P	*Past and Present*
Peacey	J. Peacey (ed.), *The Regicides and the Execution of Charles I*, Basingstoke, 2001
Thomson	A. Thomson (ed.), *The Impact of the First Civil War on Hertfordshire, 1642–7*, Hertfordshire Record Society, xxiv, 2007
TRHS	*Transactions of the Royal Historical Society*
War and Society	B. Bond and I. Roy (eds), *War and Society*, i, London, 1975
Woodhouse	A.S.P. Woodhouse, *Puritanism and Liberty*, London, 1938

FOREWORD

Why yet another book on the English civil war? My aim in writing this has been to produce something for students and interested general readers that is both brief and clear. Recent studies have become not only more and more detailed but also larger: one weighed in at 1.5 kilos. The reader risks becoming lost in a maze of detail, and it becomes harder and harder to maintain a grasp of the big picture. The reader's problems are made worse by the fact that this is an exceptionally complicated period. Although the civil war is usually seen (in England) in terms of two sides, at times there were a daunting number of other players, including the Scots, the Irish, the army and the people of England (and especially of London). At some points things happened and perspectives changed with alarming and disorienting rapidity. If it is hard to judge at times where contemporaries stood in relation to one another, they were often just as confused themselves. Moreover, as the 1640s wore on, events unfolded in ways which contemporaries had not expected and did not want. This makes it especially necessary to avoid being seduced by hindsight, to assume that everything logically led to the trial and execution of the king; as we shall see, these were in fact highly improbable outcomes.

To produce a clear and comprehensible narrative some things have had to be left out. I generally pass over in silence the many negotiations which did not lead to anything. I also omit any discussion of historiography (which I would not do with my students). What I am offering is my own synthesis.

Others may disagree with it, but it has the merit of being (in my eyes at least) coherent and accurate. Finally, since the mid-1980s or so a 'three kingdoms' approach to the subjects has become almost a matter of political correctness. In this book I concentrate unashamedly on England: events in Scotland and Ireland are mentioned only insofar as they had an impact on events in England.

John Miller

I

A PEACEABLE NATION

On the morning of 10 January 1642, Charles I, his wife, Henrietta Maria, and their children left Whitehall Palace by barge for Hampton Court. For more than two weeks the palace had been besieged by angry Londoners and defended by disbanded soldiers, whom the citizens derisively called 'cavaliers'. Five days earlier Charles had gone to Guildhall, in the City, where his Parliament had taken refuge, claiming that it was no longer safe at Westminster; he had returned to Whitehall amid jeers and catcalls and the lord mayor, who escorted him, was manhandled. Although the anger and violence had reached a peak in the last two weeks, there had been sporadic but sometimes serious violence in the capital for more than eighteen months. In June 1640 Lambeth Palace had been attacked by a furious crowd, eager to seize, and possibly lynch, the archbishop of Canterbury. The violence and disorder in London were replicated in the provinces, where it seemed that all order had broken down. As the royal party made its way upstream, the king and queen had ample time to ponder the spirit of rebellion which seemed to have gripped the English people. Their sense of disorientation was increased when they arrived at Hampton Court, only to discover that no preparations had been made to receive them and no linen or furniture had been sent from Whitehall. That night, which was bitterly cold, the king, queen and children all huddled together in the same bed.

For those who witnessed the disorders of 1640–2, and the four years of civil war that followed, it must have appeared that the English people had cast off all respect for law and authority. The events of the 1640s, indeed, led to the perception across Europe that the English were a violent and disorderly people. In many ways, this perception was seriously awry. The last civil war in England had ended with the triumph of Henry VII over Richard III in 1485. The last significant popular rebellion had been an agrarian revolt in the East Midlands in 1607. The English had a reputation for being irascible and quarrelsome, especially when drunk, but in general they showed a predisposition to obey authority. This was just as well, because the state's means of coercion were pitifully inadequate. One of the main problems of explaining the English civil war is that it occurred within a society which, far from teetering on the edge of anarchy, was profoundly orderly and stable.

The problem of explaining the civil wars of the 1640s is made greater by the fact that they were on a scale quite unmatched in English history, before or since. The civil wars of the Middle Ages generally involved a few great nobles, their retainers and vassals, and were often triggered by contests for the crown: 'kings' games and for the more part played on scaffolds'. Battle armies were normally numbered in hundreds rather than thousands and their impact was localized; larger-scale revolts, like those led by Wat Tyler or Jack Cade, were generally peasant protests against misgovernment. By contrast the civil wars of the 1640s affected the greater part of England and Wales, and as many as a third of the adult male population was in arms at some time. The death toll, in battle or from related causes, was probably higher, as a percentage of the population, than in the First World War. The civil wars of the 1640s also brought about far more dramatic changes, and upheavals, than those of the Middle Ages. The civil wars of the twelfth, or the fifteenth century were fought to decide who should be king. In the 1640s a king was defeated by a Parliament claiming to act for his people, and then tried and executed. The monarchy was abolished, along with the House of Lords (an integral part of Parliament since it began in the thirteenth century), and government of the national church by bishops (which had been established long before the Norman Conquest). The political dominance of the landed aristocracy was challenged and then overthrown by men of humbler origins, notably the New Model Army, which was the dominant force in the nation for more than a decade. This was accompanied by an unprecedented freedom to preach and publish, which many condemned as destroying all established order and authority, and turning the world upside down.

Much of the old order – the monarchy, the Lords, the bishops – was restored, starting in 1660, but for many the restored old order seemed fragile, and there were to be more occasions (in 1679–83, 1688–9 and 1715–16) when another civil war seemed more than possible. This sense of fragility led later generations to try to analyse the reasons for the breakdown of the 1640s. Few openly suggested that there was much seriously wrong with the institutions through which England had been governed for centuries: the monarchy, Parliament, the common law, the Church (although the last had needed to be cleansed of popish corruption in the sixteenth century). Observers preferred to blame small, but influential groups. Thomas Hobbes focused his ire on Puritan preachers and the universities where they were trained. Edward Hyde, created earl of Clarendon at the Restoration, blamed a small group of ambitious and politically motivated men, but also accepted that Charles I, whom he had served in the 1640s, had on occasion made mistakes. A more general tendency, after 1660, was to cast all the odium on the Parliamentarians and those seen as their lineal successors – Presbyterians and other religious Dissenters, Low Church clergymen and Whigs. The lineal heirs of the Royalists – High Church Anglicans and Tories – constantly accused their opponents of being as anti-monarchical as those responsible for Charles I's execution. This view was by no means confined to politicians: well into the eighteenth century Tory crowds on election days chanted 'down with the Roundheads, down with the Rump'. Stimulated in part by the publication of Clarendon's *History of the Rebellion*, the cult of the Royal Martyr, and of divine right monarchy, reached its zenith at the beginning of the eighteenth century, in the reign of Queen Anne. The memory was kept alive by the legal requirement to keep 30 January, the anniversary of the regicide, as a day of fasting and humiliation. High Church parsons revelled in the opportunity to instil in their flocks a proper sense of the sinfulness of resistance to lawful authority and the 'sacrilege' of king-killing.

If the civil wars were such a cataclysm, and had such a lasting impact, surely contemporaries must have seen them coming? There is very little indication that they did. The greatest fear of the English political nation in the early seventeenth century was that their kings planned to set themselves up as absolute monarchs, like those of France and Spain. James I and Charles I were perceived as seeking to undermine the personal liberty and property rights of their subjects, guaranteed to them for centuries by the common law (and especially the right to trial by jury) and by Parliament, without whose consent new laws could not be introduced and taxes could not be imposed. Parliament also acted as an invaluable mouthpiece for the grievances of the subject. Between 1629 and 1640 Parliament did not meet, but Clarendon later wrote (perhaps with the benefit of hindsight) that in the 1630s England 'enjoyed the greatest calm and the fullest measure of felicity that any people in any age for so long time together have been blessed with'.[1] He may have exaggerated the level of happiness. There was little sign of contentment among Puritans fleeing to freedom in the 'howling wilderness' of New England, or fen dwellers deprived of their ancient common rights by predatory syndicates of drainers, with the full backing of the king, or those fined large sums for unwittingly breaching long-forgotten laws. But much of this discontent was confined to diaries and alehouse muttering, or to relatively small groups of people. Superficially at least, England was a peaceful country, especially when compared to its continental neighbours, locked into the bloody struggles of the Thirty Years' War.

England had not always been so peaceful. The fifteenth century had seen protracted struggles for the crown, the Wars of the Roses. The Tudor regime faced a series of rebellions, from the rising led by Perkin Warbeck in 1487 to the abortive putsch of the earl of Essex in 1601. But most of these 'rebellions' had neither been directed against the monarch nor were designed to change the ruler. Many were demonstrations, or protests, appealing to the monarch for justice against the misdeeds of landlords, or the threat of religious change. Compared with France, there were few revolts against taxes and tax collection, for the simple reason that in the century before 1640 the poor paid virtually no taxes. (This was to change with a vengeance in the 1640s.) In addition, under Elizabeth a system of poor relief was put in place which provided enough of a safety net to prevent the poorest from starving to death, although many went hungry in years of dearth. The protagonists in even the largest and bloodiest tax revolts in France were careful to proclaim their loyalty to the king, crying 'Long live the king without the salt tax'. English rebels were generally less violent, and there was also one other major contrast between England and France in the sixteenth century. France suffered a series of religious civil wars, which eventually became linked to disputes as to who should be king. England did not suffer such wars, even though from Henry VIII's death in 1547 to the execution of Mary Queen of Scots in 1587, there was always a possible alternative monarch of the opposite religion to the reigning monarch. On the face of it, this would seem a perfect recipe for a religious civil war, but none ensued. The Wars of the Roses had had their origins in competition for the crown. Henry VIII's three children succeeded one another in an orderly fashion. The right of succession of Edward VI, then Mary, then Elizabeth was barely challenged: the attempt to install Lady Jane Grey as queen in 1553 lasted only nine days. Moreover, those rebels who had a dynastic agenda – Wyatt in 1554, the Northern earls in 1569 – were careful to keep it secret.

At some time, then, between the deaths of Richard III and Henry VIII, the monarchy had become more secure, and challenging the reigning monarch had become unacceptable. A key development here was a change in the relationship between the king and the nobility. In mid-seventeenth-century France there were still nobles, like the prince de Condé, who could mobilize whole regions against the king. There were few such magnates in England even in the fifteenth century, and they were mostly found in the North, where the king relied on them to guard the Scottish border. Elsewhere, few nobles could raise large armies, though most had enough loyal servants, tenants and retainers to maintain a rudimentary level of law and order, and to ensure that at least some of the king's commands were carried out in the localities. This loyalty was sustained partly by the granting of rewards in return for service and partly through an honour culture which emphasized a man's obligations to his lord in parallel with, or even above, his loyalty to the king. The Tudors were adamant that such dual loyalties were unacceptable: all subjects owed allegiance first and foremost to the crown. They were able to insist on this because the inherent power of the nobility was waning. Their military role, so crucial to their wealth and power during the Hundred Years' War, became less and less important. Changes in warfare reduced the importance of cavalry, the traditional métier of nobles and knights, and increased the importance of infantry, fortifications and artillery. The service in war which had once made the nobles indispensable to the crown became less and less necessary.

The nobles were also losing much of their power over men. In the past their large estates had given them a numerous tenantry and many, especially in the North, had made a point of renting farms to the same families, which over the generations created a strong bond of loyalty between lord and man. Tenants, household servants and client gentry (lesser landowners) together formed a body of men who could serve either in armed conflict (local feuds as well as actual war) or in local administration and justice (for example as jurors). In return for this service the lord could offer protection – very necessary under a weak king – but also reward, either from his own resources or from the crown: in return for making the king's rule effective in the localities, the nobles expected him to provide rewards (lands, jobs, places in the Church) for their kinsmen, clients and followers. This was a rough and ready form of governance, but it could be found across much of Europe (including Scotland) in the sixteenth and seventeenth centuries and beyond. In England, however, it began to break down under the Tudors.

Rising prices forced landlords to find ways of increasing their income from rents, or face a significant decline in their standard of living. As the population was rising, tenants were competing for farms, and landlords could demand higher rents, but granting tenancies to the highest bidder undermined the mutual loyalties built up over generations between aristocratic families and their tenants. Even in the far North, the earls of Northumberland were putting commercial considerations before traditional loyalties by the 1560s, and they paid the price. In the fifteenth century, their tenants would follow them anywhere, even in rebellion against the crown. In 1569 the earl was able to mobilize some of his tenants in the rising of the Northern earls, but by appealing to their Catholicism rather than their loyalty to his family. In 1642, when the earl summoned his tenants to serve him in the civil war, it was said that they blockaded him in Alnwick Castle.[2]

The crown, too, played its part in undermining the power of the nobility. Henry VIII ruthlessly eliminated anyone who might stake the slightest claim to the throne. More generally, the Tudors set out to ensure that royal justice prevailed throughout the land. In the Middle Ages, magnates often distorted the proceedings of law courts, through their influence over judges, magistrates, jurors and sheriffs (who selected juries). This influence could be comparatively subtle, it could be direct and brutal. Under the Tudors magnates accused of perverting the course of justice were summoned before the Court of Star Chamber, which consisted of the king's privy council and one or two judges. It did not use juries or the normal procedures and personnel of common law, and so was much less susceptible to noble influence than local courts were. It was increasingly seen as effective in protecting the relatively humble against the powerful; as such it became popular with litigants. Great landowners came to realize that there was no point in trying to influence legal proceedings – or to take the law into their own hands and settle disputes by force. It was not only risky for them to resort to force: they also lost much of their ability to do so. As their military role declined, they no longer needed to keep substantial bodies of household retainers and their influence over their clients declined, since these found it more effective to approach the crown directly. As England became more orderly, as law enforcement became more effective, disputes were settled not by force but by law. Now that they no longer needed to fear powerful neighbours, great landowners stopped building castles – Kenilworth, early in Elizabeth's reign, was about the last – instead building unfortified palaces, like Burghley House, Longleat or Audley End.

In the fifteenth century English society was still militarized, in the sense that war shaped the culture and attitudes of the nobility and armed force was an essential component of their power; this is why noblemen played a central role in civil wars and struggles for the crown. By the end of Elizabeth's reign, this was no longer so. Where armies had once been formed of the personal followings of great nobles, the basic form of military service was now the militia – an essentially civilian force, under-resourced and under-trained, in which peasants and craftsmen provided the rank and file, the gentry served as officers and the commander in each county was the lord lieutenant, usually a peer. The organization and funding of the militia was laid down by Acts of Parliament, and those who served in it did so by virtue of commissions from the crown. When Essex rebelled in 1601, his followers were cavalrymen who had served with him in the wars in Ireland. They had fine swords and horses, but to stand any chance of succeeding they needed the support of the muskets of the London militia – which they failed to secure. In the early seventeenth century, the English nobility was probably the least militarized in Europe. Over-mighty noblemen with large armies played a central role in the Frondes, the civil wars in France between 1648 and 1652. English noblemen no longer had that sort of military power. The influence that they exercised in the civil wars stemmed mainly from their activities in Parliament and the administration, not from their military might or regional power.

The English civil war was thus a new type of conflict in that the role, and especially the military role, of the nobility was limited – far more limited than in the Dutch revolt, the French wars of religion or the Frondes. In addition, there was no real argument in early seventeenth-century England as to who should be king. There had been some fears of opposition to James I's accession in 1603, but none about that of his successor in 1625: and by 1640 Charles had two sons to carry on the dynasty.

There was another important difference. In both the Netherlands and France, the component provinces retained a strong sense of their own identity, institutions and privileges, which they defended stubbornly against the efforts of their rulers to extend their authority. The people of Languedoc saw the people of Normandy as foreigners, who did not even speak the same language. In the same way the Catalans rebelled against the rule of their Castilian overlords in Madrid. The major kings of continental Europe ruled over a disparate variety of provinces, territories and kingdoms. The kings of Spain ruled – or tried to rule – the various kingdoms of the Iberian peninsula (including Portugal), Naples, Sicily, Milan and a substantial part of the Netherlands. These lands had been acquired piecemeal over the centuries, and often had nothing in common except that they happened to have the same ruler. England had been ruled as an entity since before the Norman Conquest. It had a single system of law (Luxembourg had over a hundred) and, since the thirteenth century, a single representative institution, Parliament. Its people spoke the same language (except in Cornwall). Even the union with Wales, in the 1530s, did little to disrupt this sense of unity. The Welsh generally accepted the English system of local government and English law. Welsh landowners were happy to seek election to the English Parliament. The Welsh language survived – it was indeed the language of the majority in the mid-seventeenth century – but this caused little friction since the English showed little inclination to eradicate it; the Bible and Prayer Book were translated into Welsh, which became the language of religion. This meant that the impact of Protestantism on Wales was comparatively limited: English-speaking clergymen could do little to instruct their Welsh-speaking flocks, and traditional Catholic and perhaps pre-Christian practices continued alongside the official services. On the other hand, the Tudors' Welsh origins and the perception that the Stuarts, as Scots, were fellow-Celts inspired among the Welsh a fierce loyalty to their monarchs.

Reference to the Dutch revolt and the French wars of religion offer a reminder that in sixteenth- and seventeenth-century Europe religious differences were a major feature of civil wars and added substantially to their bitterness and brutality. But, as has already been noted, there was no war of religion in England in the sixteenth century. The nation generally acquiesced with the breach with Rome under Henry VIII, the attempt to establish Protestantism under Edward VI, the reversion to Catholicism under Mary and the re-establishment of Protestantism under Elizabeth. Catholic crucifixes and vestments were confiscated under Edward, restored under Mary, and confiscated again under Elizabeth. Parliament, the representative of the nation, carried through all the changes, back and forth, with surprisingly little demur. Catholic England put up some stiff resistance, in the Pilgrimage of Grace of 1536, the Western Rising of 1549, and the rising of the Northern earls, but none of these was a rising against the ruling monarch: all blamed evil counsellors for giving misleading advice. There was plenty of religious argument, often acrimonious, but it was all within the context of loyalty to the crown: from the 1540s a series of homilies on obedience, read regularly in churches, hammered away at the point that active resistance to the monarch – God's anointed – was an offence against God. Most Catholics, who in theory owed spiritual allegiance to the pope, proclaimed their unswerving loyalty to the crown. As Protestantism slowly put down deeper roots, in the reign of Elizabeth, most (but not all) of the fiercest debates took place between Protestants, who agreed, however, that Elizabeth's safety and survival were vital for the survival of English Protestantism. For much of James I's reign, different strains of Protestantism coexisted relatively peacefully within the Church of England under a king who proclaimed his commitment to peace. A war of religion in England seemed most unlikely.

All of the above would suggest that a civil war in England in the 1640s was highly improbable, far more improbable than a century before. And yet there was no civil war in mid-Tudor England but a cataclysmic war in the 1640s. To explain why this happened we need to extend our analysis. First, while England may have been a peaceful, homogeneous and comparatively orderly kingdom, the same could not be said of the Stuarts' other two kingdoms, Scotland and Ireland. The crowns of England and Scotland had been united in 1603, when James VI of Scotland became also James I of England. Compared with England, Scotland was an impoverished nation, with a high level of violence and disorder. Power lay primarily in the hands of the nobility, whose hold over the peasantry was based on physical force and the ability to offer protection, reinforced by private law courts which ensured that (in contrast to England) peasants could not seek legal redress against their lords. If James VI managed to establish a modicum of order in Scotland, it was because he became skilled in managing its fractious nobility. The rule of law was at best rudimentary: the first published digest of Scottish law appeared in 1681. The most ordered parts of Scotland were the central Lowlands and the north-east, but even there brigandage and feuding continued throughout the sixteenth century. The Highlands remained a lawless zone: a tribal or clan society, Gaelic-speaking and largely Catholic, from which raiding parties came down into the Lowlands even in the early seventeenth century. The Borders, too, remained a violent frontier region, even after an unaccustomed outbreak of peace between England and Scotland under Elizabeth and James I. If English society was no longer militarized, Scottish society most certainly remained so.

That said, there were forces making for greater order and stability in Scotland. The nobles might be capricious and turbulent, but they respected the monarchy and the rewards that even an impoverished king was able to give them. The lesser landowners, the lairds, lacking the military power of the nobles, had a vested interest in peace and order, as did lawyers and the people of the towns. But perhaps the most powerful force in Scotland, other than the nobility, was the Kirk, the Church of Scotland. While in England the Reformation had been directed by the crown, in Scotland it had been carried through while James VI was a minor. Whereas the Church of England was controlled by its supreme head, the monarch, who appointed the bishops who governed it, the Kirk was independent of the crown. Its government was Presbyterian: each parish had a kirk session, consisting of the minister and lay elders, who maintained moral discipline. Representatives of the parishes were elected to regional synods and then the national General Assembly, which laid down rules of governance for the Kirk as a whole and secured the support of the secular authorities in maintaining moral discipline. With their combination of moral authority as pastors and effective disciplinary powers, the Presbyterian clergy exercised a control over the ordinary people of Scotland, comparable to (but very different from) that of the nobility.

Scotland was thus a more violent country than England, and a more divided one: there was no real parallel in England to the sharp division between Highland and Lowland, or Gaelic and Scots (a language different from English, but with numerous and increasing similarities). The differences were even starker in Ireland. Although the English had conquered Ireland in the twelfth century, English rule had remained relatively superficial, largely confined to the Pale (the area around Dublin) until the sixteenth century. Then the breach with Rome and the establishment of Protestantism in England made the staunch Catholicism of Ireland a potential problem for England's rulers. If the Irish maintained their loyalty to the pope, who in 1570 excommunicated Elizabeth and declared her subjects absolved from their allegiance, there would be a constant threat that any Catholic enemy of England (which at this time meant Spain) could use Ireland as a springboard from which to attack England from the rear. This potential security problem led English soldiers and officials in Ireland to advocate a radical and drastic transformation of its government and people.

The gulf between the English in Ireland and the Gaelic Irish was based on much more than differences of religion: here was a confrontation between two different civilizations. Gaelic Ireland, like Highland Scotland, was a tribal society, in which clan chiefs wielded near absolute power over the peasantry, but also commanded a strong and resilient loyalty. They offered protection, and occasionally plunder, in return for tribute (mainly agricultural produce) and service. This was a mainly pastoral society, in which wealth was measured in cattle, rather than the ownership of land. Settlements were small and often temporary; many moved with their herds to the higher grazing during the summer months. In Gaelic areas, especially Ulster, towns were few and very small even in 1600. When a chief died, he was replaced by an adult male member of his family who was strong, or cunning, enough to defeat his rivals. Disputes were adjudicated by chiefs or their henchmen according to rules which English officials found incomprehensible. In the eyes of the English, the Irish were primitive, barbarians. The peasants were slaves to their chiefs and to the Catholic clergy, who took the bulk of what they produced, leaving them wretchedly poor. They had no incentive to produce more, because if they did the chiefs and priests would take more. Whereas the English saw Scotland as bleak and barren, 'the fag end of the creation',[3] they saw Ireland as potentially fertile and prosperous, but made backward by the bovine submission of the peasantry and the predatory greed of their chiefs. If Ireland was ever to cease to pose a threat to England, it needed to be modernized, indeed civilized. Its economy should be revived by the expansion of arable farming, manufactures, trade and towns. English forms of government should be introduced, with an impartial system of laws and law courts to enable the peasants to secure their rights against their lords. Property ownership should be formalized through written documents, title deeds, rather than an unstable mixture of custom and possession through brute force. And Protestantism and the English language should replace Catholicism and Gaelic.[4]

For this vision of Anglicization – set out with brutal frankness by the poet Edmund Spenser – to become reality, it would be necessary to transfer the ownership of land from Irishmen to Englishmen. The Irish people could be converted to English ways only by having before them the example of English hard work, organization and modernity. Starting (ironically) in the reign of the Catholic Queen Mary, there were a series of schemes to establish 'plantations', vesting land in English proprietors who would bring over English farmers and artisans. For this to succeed, it was necessary to take land away from Catholics, for which some sort of legal pretext was necessary: the most significant plantation of Elizabeth's reign, in Munster, followed an abortive rebellion in 1579–83, after which land was confiscated from some of the rebels, but also from others who had played no part. The process of plantation depended ultimately on military force. Soldiers were in the vanguard of the process and dealt brutally with those who stood in their way. In the end, the English goaded the Irish into a revolt which turned into the Nine Years' War. It was fought with great ruthlessness on both sides. Atrocities were frequent, large areas were devastated and the Munster plantation was destroyed. More and more men and money were devoted to the war effort until at last the leaders of the rebellion surrendered, on terms, a few days after Elizabeth's death in 1603.

At the heart of early seventeenth-century Ireland lay an unbridgeable ethnic and religious divide between Gaelic Irish and English Protestant. Not everyone fitted neatly into these categories. There were also Catholics of English descent, the Old English, who thought of themselves as English, and a growing number of Scots who made the short sea crossing to Ulster. But English Protestants in Ireland chose to explain the problems of Ireland in terms of English against Irish, Protestant against Catholic. They depicted the Catholic Irish, Gaelic and Old English, as rebellious and irreconcilable, so that Ireland could be pacified and 'civilized' only if the power of the Catholic landowners was broken. Between 1603 and 1640, they engineered the transfer of extensive tracts of land from Catholic (mostly Gaelic) to Protestant, taking advantage of the 'treason' of two of the great Gaelic lords of Ulster and the difficulty of many Irish landowners in demonstrating their title to their lands in terms acceptable to English law. As more and more land passed from Catholic to Protestant, so Catholics were increasingly excluded from public office and from Parliament. But this was a slow process. In 1640 the proportion of land in Protestant hands, though much increased since 1603, was still only around 40 per cent. The power which Catholic lords – even those who had been dispossessed – still exercised over the peasantry remained considerable. Violence and brigandage remained at a level akin to that found in the Scottish Highlands. The struggle for Ireland gradually moved in favour of the English Protestants, but their victory was by no means assured. The resentment of the Irish smouldered, and they waited for an opportunity to recover what they had lost.

Scotland and Ireland, then, created potential problems for the English kings of a different order from those they faced in England. These were violent, militarized societies, ethnically and religiously divided: it is significant that both rebelled – the Scots in 1637, the Irish in 1641 – before civil war broke out in England. Indeed, it is unlikely that the civil disobedience and tax refusal which spread through England in 1639 and especially 1640 would have happened without the prospect that the Scots would force the king to reverse his policies.

And yet the English were perhaps not quite as docile as they appeared. Foreigners found them rude, aggressive and violent. Homicide levels were much higher than they are now, although this owed something to primitive medical techniques: injuries acquired in pub brawls could subsequently prove fatal. Nevertheless, the English chose to obey laws and pay the few taxes imposed on them. And this was to some extent a matter of choice. The crown's powers of coercion were flimsy: Charles I had no standing army or police force, and only a minuscule professional bureaucracy. Government and law enforcement in the localities depended on unpaid local people: parish officers, magistrates, jurors. They participated in government because it was their duty as citizens, and by participating they gained a sense of ownership and empowerment. Many held office only temporarily, often for a year at a time, and even those who did not knew that to perform effectively they needed the acceptance of their fellow villagers or townspeople. Urban governors were expected to regulate the markets, maintain the streets to an acceptable level, preserve law and order, relieve the deserving poor and punish the 'loose, idle and disorderly'. If they did so, they could expect cooperation and obedience from their fellow citizens: if not, they might face disobedience and serious disorder.

The English accepted the need for ordered government, functioning according to known rules. Nowhere is this seen more clearly that in the Berkshire village of Swallowfield, which in 1596 drew up what was in effect a village constitution, setting up a government to deal with problems like poverty, drunkenness and disorder.[5] But submission to authority was not unconditional. It rested on certain expectations – tacit expectations, perhaps, but no less real for that. Village constables and town magistrates had to conduct themselves in a manner acceptable to their neighbours. The obedience owed to kings, their officials and their laws rested on similar, but more extensive expectations. The governance of the kingdom, as well as that of village or town, rested on participation by the governed and that participation implied that both parties followed certain ground rules. Running through the English constitution was a sense of reciprocity. Kings were expected to govern for the good of their people. Their essential tasks were the defence of the realm, law and order, maintaining true religion and promoting prosperity and well-being: all of which would help the people to live ordered, peaceful lives and to enjoy their personal liberty and property. This reciprocity was seen most clearly in Parliament. Medieval kings across Europe had developed representative assemblies as a means of securing consent to taxation and new laws, thus making it easier to collect taxes and have laws obeyed. The English Parliament saw its role as helping the monarch to govern, by providing new laws to deal with new problems (for example the growing incidence of poverty in Elizabeth's reign) and voting taxes to meet those essential functions of government which the king could not pay for out of his landed estates and other resources. The most significant of these were import duties, voted to each Tudor monarch for life, which were supposed to pay for the navy, and one-off taxes on land to pay for war. Parliament's role was not to govern, but to help the king to govern. This also involved making the king aware of misgovernment by bringing the grievances of the people to his attention. It was hoped that, once he was aware of grievances, he would, as a just king, remedy them. If he did not, it would be natural to see Parliament's twin functions – voting laws and taxes on one hand, presenting grievances on the other – as linked, so that taxation ('supply') could become conditional, at least implicitly, on the redress of grievances.

In many respects the English were an obedient and orderly people. They respected the law, in part because they played such a large part in enforcing it. They obeyed government because they helped to define its tasks and fulfil them. If they failed to secure justice from the courts, or the government, they might rebel or riot. But the brutal suppression of rebellions by the Tudors, and the Church's endless harping on the impiety of resistance, gradually got across the hard lesson that this was not an admissible form of action. The last significant rebellion was that of the Northern earls in 1569; when an Oxfordshire man called on the peasantry to rise up against the landowners in 1596, only three people turned up. Riots continued much longer, but these were not directed against the king or those in authority, but were demonstrations against failures to take steps to prevent dearth, or attacks on common rights by individual landlords. Paradoxically, riots were usually expressions of respect for custom and law, and were usually disciplined and non-violent. (One exception was in the Fens, where Flemish drainage workers were beaten up: as they spoke no English, violence was the only language that they might understand.) In short, the generally peaceable and law-abiding behaviour of the English did not mean that they showed the fatalistic submission of Scottish or Irish peasants. It was an informed and, ultimately, conditional submission – conditional on their rulers, and especially the king, behaving in ways which they regarded as just or fair. If the habit of rebellion died out in the sixteenth century, the habit of riot did not, and it was driven by a fierce sense of justice. If riots were rarely directed against the monarch, that was because most monarchs were restrained by conscience or common sense from stretching their subjects' loyalty and obedience too far. That was to change under Charles I.

2

CHARLES I

England was not an easy country to rule: the English, through their participation in government and law enforcement, had developed strong feelings about what was legal, just and fair. However, their deep-seated willingness to obey authority, and their aversion to active resistance, made it difficult for even the most incompetent or malevolent king to goad them into revolt. It says much for Charles I's record as king that he managed to do just this. In explaining the outbreak of the civil war, we need to address two separate but related questions. First, why were so many of Charles's subjects driven to a point where they were prepared, despite their principles, to take up arms against him? Second, why, despite the manifold abuses of his regime and his proven record of deceit and duplicity, were enough people prepared to fight for the king and so make civil war possible? The answer to this second question lies in the years 1640–2: there was no prospect of civil war in 1640 because the king did not have the necessary support. The aim of this chapter is to show why he was so isolated in 1640 and why many of his subjects welcomed a foreign invasion.

Unlike his father, who wrote extensively on political ideas, Charles I was not driven by any clearly formulated view of monarchy. He was a man of simplistic assumptions, not carefully thought out theories. For him, the task of kings was to rule, the duty of subjects was to obey. For subjects to question the dictates of government was at best misguided, and at worst subversive and even treasonous. Charles's mind functioned in terms of simple polar opposites: good and bad, right and wrong, loyal and disloyal. Confident that he had his subjects' best interests at heart, he expected them to acquiesce unquestioningly in whatever he commanded. He was answerable to God for his conduct as king, not to Parliament and certainly not to his people as a whole. His father had once remarked that he did not know why his predecessors had allowed such a body as Parliament to come into being: it never occurred to either James or Charles that it might be a useful institution, which could assist in the business of government. But it could be useful only if the king engaged in dialogue with its members and was prepared to make at least a show of taking their advice. Neither James nor Charles was prepared to be swayed by a body that both saw as seeking to undermine the authority of the crown. Both accused some members of seeking 'popularity', of trying to use the fickle multitude to undermine the government. The stormy history of the five Parliaments that sat between 1621 and 1629 first and foremost reflected failures of policy and communication on the part of the two kings, but their fears that MPs were threatening their legitimate authority were not altogether fanciful. In 1621 the Commons revived the practice of impeachment (prosecution by the House of Commons before the House of Lords), which had last been used in the fifteenth century. Initially it was used against men accused of corruption, but it was also used to attack senior ministers and the favourite of both kings, the duke of Buckingham. At the same time, the Commons set up investigative committees, which claimed the right to summon witnesses, demand to see documents, and imprison those who refused to testify. Together these measures restricted the king's freedom to choose his advisers, and sought to probe confidential areas of government. In 1625 the Commons refused to grant the incoming king the usual import duties for life. The Commons probably intended to use this grant as a lever to persuade the king to abandon what they regarded as unlawful taxes. From the king's point of view they were starving him of money (especially as he had just embarked on a war against Spain, at their request) as a means of extorting concessions. In 1628 the Commons denied that the king's privy council had the power to commit people to gaol without showing cause, even though it had done so repeatedly in the past, notably when imprisoning those accused of involvement in the Gunpowder Plot in 1605.

Charles saw these innovations (for that is what they were) by the Commons as evidence of a conspiracy of a smallish group of ambitious politicians to pry into his government and strip him of his powers. But the Commons' behaviour showed few signs of the aggression and ambition ascribed to them by the king. Instead the atmosphere was one of panic, even despair. Both James and Charles collected taxes without the consent of Parliament. James found a legal pretext to collect additional import duties (impositions); Charles also collected the regular import duties (tonnage and poundage) without Parliament's consent after the Commons had refused to vote them for life in 1625. Having failed to secure a grant of taxation in 1626, he initiated a forced loan, demanding that his wealthier subjects lend him money, and imprisoning without trial some of those who refused. When some of these demanded to be brought to court, their lawyers were told that they had been imprisoned by a special order of the privy council. In addition, Star Chamber, once used to bring to book over-mighty subjects, was now used to punish critics of the regime, notably those who published unlicensed pamphlets. Together these developments conjured up a bleak prospect. Charles seemed to be seeking to emancipate himself from the need for his subjects' consent, and dismantling the protection that the law traditionally gave to personal liberty and property. The ancient liberties of England, and the institution of Parliament itself, seemed to be under threat. Nor were such fears unduly paranoid. A government minister warned of the dire consequences that would ensue if Parliament failed to comply with the king's wishes, while the king told the Commons that they should not think he was threatening them, as he scorned to threaten any but his equals.

Charles had decided by 1626 that he would be better off without Parliament; yet he was locked into a war – catastrophically mismanaged – for which he needed money. In 1629, however, as the war meandered towards its end, he felt able to dissolve Parliament. He informed his people that he had been misunderstood and misrepresented, and that he intended to embark on a period without Parliament, in which his subjects could learn to appreciate the benevolence of his government, free of the carping of self-seeking politicians. Many of his people, however, saw little in his rule that was benevolent. In the Fens, consortia of drainers used legal chicanery and strong-arm tactics to deprive the fenmen of their ancient rights, while the king made sure that they could receive no redress through the courts; those who rioted were hauled up before Star Chamber. Much the same happened when the king's City friends cleared forests and seized mining rights in the Forest of Dean and the West Country. Many landowners were fined for encroaching on long-forgotten royal forests, or for failing to come to court to be knighted, as required by an ancient law. The Corporation of London was fined £70,000, for failing to fulfil all the obligations in its contract for developing the plantation of Londonderry. Civil servants were threatened with a major reorganization of office-holding, which was graciously abandoned when they clubbed together to give the king money. Monopolies, which had caused outrage under James I, were revived to make money for the king's courtiers and their friends in the City – and for the king himself. Many of these money-making scams affected only specific groups of people, but the cumulative effect was to create a perception of the king's regime as predatory and corrupt. Yet while the victims might feel that they had been unjustly treated, the crown's demands were lawful, insofar as they were upheld by the courts and were often based on ancient laws that had never been revoked.

There was one fiscal device, however, which was much more generally resented. For centuries the crown had, in an emergency, levied ship money on coastal areas, to enable it to hire ships for defence against the threat of invasion or pirates. Getting areas to pay for their own defence was well established – for example in the county militia rates. In the 1630s, the king's legal advisers argued that, if the king judged that the national interest required it, he could demand that the whole kingdom should pay ship money. Soon demands for payment were issued each year, creating the interesting concept of a regular annual emergency. When the case of one of the richest landowners in Buckinghamshire, John Hampden, was heard in 1637 – he had refused to pay – his counsel argued that ship money was essentially a tax and the proper place for taxes to be imposed was in Parliament. The king's lawyers argued that there were ample precedents for the king ordering levies of ship money and it was up to the king, not his subjects, to judge whether there was an emergency. The judges found for the king and ship money continued to be collected.

The ship money trial highlighted a growing unease about the king's misuse of the law. It was not so much that the judges (appointed by the king) wilfully misinterpreted the law, but rather that they preferred to focus on the letter of the law, and on specific precedents, rather than on its spirit. They did so partly because that was the way common lawyers tended to think, considering precedents rather than wider principles, but also because what was really at issue was the king's use of his judgement and of his prerogative. The judges were not prepared

to question the king's integrity, any more than their predecessors had wished to question James I's claim that he was
collecting impositions in order to stem the flow of imports into
England, and not to raise money. The judges were the king's
judges, the law courts were the king's courts, and it was a principle of the common law that the king could do no wrong
(although his ministers could). On top of all this, the king's law
officers were confident, when the Hampden case came to court,
that the king would win, because they had earlier asked the
judges whether it would be legal to extend ship money to inland
counties, if the king judged that it was in the national interest.
Most of the judges had agreed that it would, but this practice of
presenting hypothetical questions to the judges raised significant issues. In deciding in general terms that a levy like ship
money was legal, the judges were in effect usurping the role of
Parliament and granting money to the king; and although the
king's lawyers might claim that it was a local rate rather than a
tax, it was a tax to all intents and purposes. So if the judges
would change the law and (in effect) grant taxes, why should the
king need to call Parliament? And if the common law courts
could not protect the liberty and property of the subject, who
could? To make matters worse, Star Chamber (which did not
use juries or follow the procedural rules of common law) was
increasingly used against those regarded by the king as dissidents or subversives: not just rioting fenmen, but also those
protesting in print against the king's religious policy.

The Elizabethan Church of England was Protestant, but the
nature of its Protestantism was uncertain and contested. Its
confession of faith, the Thirty-nine Articles, was seen as
compatible with Calvinist theology, but its form of
government was far removed from that which prevailed in
Geneva or Scotland: it was governed by bishops who were
appointed by the crown. Some continental Calvinists did not
see this as a problem: it all depended on what sort of teaching
they provided and what sort of worship they required. From
the point of view of the 'hotter sort of Protestants', who

became known as Puritans, Elizabeth's bishops did not promote preaching, and enforced unacceptable ceremonies. In this the bishops were merely obeying the queen's orders: she distrusted preaching, preferring to keep it to a minimum, and believed that retaining some ceremonies in the Prayer Book services would make them more acceptable to religious conservatives. The struggle to carry forward the process of reformation in a Church perceived as 'but halfly reformed' was fierce and sustained, but ultimately unsuccessful. Ceremonies remained and came to be accepted and even cherished by many laypeople, if not by Puritans. The Puritans accepted defeat stoically, mystified by Elizabeth's refusal to play the part of a godly princess, and knowing that, if her regime were to be seriously destabilized, the Catholics were the most likely beneficiaries. They had higher hopes of James I, which in some ways were fulfilled. Brought up as a Calvinist, he did not share Elizabeth's distrust of preaching. Although he refused to change the Prayer Book liturgy, he tacitly allowed a diversity of practice within the Church. Open nonconformity was seen as defiance of the king's authority, but quiet deviation from the official rubric was generally tolerated. Few Puritans found James's Church intolerable, at least before the 1620s.

Nevertheless, since the 1590s conflict had been brewing within the Church. Elizabethan Protestants had seen the Church's continuities with the pre-Reformation Church, such as government by bishops and the use of ceremonies, as regrettable, but required by the queen and the law. The ceremonies required by the Prayer Book were lawful because they had been commanded by authority. Some Puritan parish ministers refrained from using them, and generally tried to make the service as Protestant as possible. To avoid any suggestion that the bread and wine in communion became anything other than bread and wine, they were distributed from a table in the middle of the aisle and the people received them sitting down – as the apostles would have done at the Last Supper. However, a group of clergy emerged who claimed that the Reformation

had gone too far. Much that was valid in Catholic worship had
been jettisoned along with what was not; the continuities with
the past were to be celebrated, not regretted. Ceremonies and
pictures helped to teach and edify the people. Preaching should
be used sparingly, since it tended to confuse or mislead simple
folk. The main focus of the service should be, not the sermon,
but communion, which should be celebrated with due pomp
and reverence, ideally before an altar.

This reaction against the Protestant Reformation was
primarily a clerical movement. It reflected in part a sense that
the Reformation had downgraded the spiritual authority of
the clergy, who now tried to reclaim their central role in cere-
monial and especially in the administering of communion.
Some at least of the claims of its protagonists were plausible.
Many laypeople found sermons confusing or boring, too
intellectual by half, and valued the features of the services
which the Puritans most deplored: not only the use of
ceremony, but the set form of service, with collective
responses which even the illiterate could learn. Puritans also
deplored the sociability associated traditionally with the
Church: church ales (to raise money for church funds), wakes
and above all Sunday sports (encouraged by James I). For
many people, Sunday was the one day when they could, after
going to church, let their hair down and have fun. But fun was
not in the Puritans' vocabulary: for them, the proper way to
spend Sunday was to discuss the sermon, read the Bible and
pray. Their moral rigour set them at odds with their neighbours, as did their theology. Following Calvin, they asserted
that God had decided since the beginning of time who was
going to be saved and who was to be damned, and there was
nothing that anyone could do about it: good works played no
part in salvation. Less intense people, living in a community,
found this doctrine either incomprehensible or unpalatable.
What sort of God would create people with the certainty that
they were going to suffer in hell for all eternity? Most people
were much more comfortable with the idea that God's main

requirement was that one should live well with one's fellow-men: indeed, the Church taught that people should receive communion only if they were in charity with their neighbours. Common prayer, communion and sociability centred on the Church emphasized the parish as a community. The Puritans' theology, and their attempts to regulate the morals of their neighbours, were essentially divisive, contrasting the godly few (themselves) with the ungodly multitude.

Until the 1620s these High Church clergy remained a minority. Some found preferment in the Church, but so did many of a more Puritan bent. James I tried to ensure that his Church remained broad: Charles I enthusiastically embraced this High Church movement, which came to be known as 'Laudian', after one of its leading figures, William Laud, who in 1633 became archbishop of Canterbury. Charles no doubt appreciated the political ideas expressed by the Laudians, who emphasized the divine nature of monarchy and the sinfulness of resistance or disobedience. But he also shared their views on the nature of worship. Charles had a highly developed aesthetic sense and was a connoisseur of fine art. Like the Laudians, he believed that worship should be dignified and orderly, but also (if it was to be truly edifying) visually beautiful: the phrase 'the beauty of holiness' summed up what Laud and Charles were trying to achieve. Church interiors needed to catch the eye and delight the senses: pictures could instruct the uneducated. Whereas the Puritans stressed the need for 'painful' (painstaking) preaching, Laud sought to reduce the number of sermons and laid stress instead on the set services in the Prayer Book; much of the instruction that the people needed could be provided by the homilies appended to it. Whereas Puritan preachers sought to awaken their listeners to an active, Bible-based piety, to bring the tepid to the boil, the Laudians saw the people as essentially passive, meekly following the leadership of the clergy. At the heart of Laudian worship was holy communion. Instead of a communion table there was to be an altar, at the east end of the church, raised so that the people could see it, and railed off, to keep out children and dogs. There, in this sacred space, the priest consecrated the bread and wine and the people came up to receive communion on their knees.

For the Puritans, all this was anathema, but it was not only Puritans who disliked Laudian worship. Those who had become accustomed to the Prayer Book services under Elizabeth and James found these innovations irritating and, still worse, popish. English Protestants were strongly anti-Catholic, and hostility to 'popery' had become a central part of English national identity. A huge literature denounced the errors of Catholic doctrine, the superstitions in Catholic worship, and the lust for wealth and power of the Catholic clergy in general, and the pope in particular. The image of Catholic practice that was purveyed in sermons and pamphlets might be seriously distorted, but it was widely accepted. For people with no first-hand experience of Catholicism, what was happening in their parish churches was, at the very least, a step towards 'popery'.

It was not just the Church's change of emphasis that caused concern: it was also the way in which Laudians came to dominate the leadership of the Church and tried to end the flexibility and diversity that had existed under James I. Laud was not one for half measures. As president of St John's College, Oxford, he had worked hard to get the students to smarten up their appearance and to keep out of undesirable alehouses; and he sought to impose a similarly thoroughgoing improvement of standards on the nation as a whole. Churches needed to be kept in good repair and decorated as appropriate. The priest needed the correct vestments; when he administered communion, the altar needed to be properly furnished, with a chalice for the wine. Many parishes fell well below his standards, partly out of sheer poverty. Communion wine was served in a tankard from the alehouse; if there was no font, babies were baptized in a bucket. For the villagers, it was the actions that were important, not the equipment. For Laud such slovenliness was an affront to God, as was the often less than reverent behaviour of some people in church – talking, sleeping, or playing with their children or dogs. The fussiness and meddling of the Laudian clergy alienated many who had no quarrel with the Prayer Book, and added to the alarm and resentment felt at 'popish' innovations in the service. An incident that typifies this resentment occurred in England's second city, Norwich. The bishop, Matthew Wren, became embroiled in a feud with the mayor and aldermen. They ceased to attend the cathedral, until Wren secured an order from the king's privy council that they had to do so. When they came, instead of the prominent seats which they had traditionally been given, they were placed in a side aisle, under a gallery, from which mischievous citizens amused themselves by spitting on their heads; someone dropped a prayer book, which broke the mayor's glasses.[1] By the time the mayor and his brethren left the building, they were seething; they boycotted the cathedral throughout the 1640s and 1650s.

For many 'Prayer Book Anglicans', the Laudian regime was distasteful and irritating. For Puritans, it was intolerable. Many emigrated to New England, or the Protestant cities of the Netherlands. Those who remained found life increasingly difficult. The leeway allowed to semi-conforming clergymen, who quietly omitted parts of the Prayer Book services, gradually disappeared. The powerful Puritan landowners and patrons of livings who had long sheltered them against the need to conform fully could no longer protect them. Orders from the king banning 'controversial' preaching prevented them from warning their flocks about the dangers they faced. A few brave individuals who did so in print were sentenced by Star Chamber to have their ears cropped. Lay Puritans found it harder and harder to find a good sermon on a Sunday. Good preachers attracted hearers from several parishes. 'Gadding to sermons' became a feature of the 1630s; families would make a day of it, bringing food and spending the latter part of the day discussing the sermon and reading their Bibles. The Puritans' rigorous morality and commitment to Sunday observance had already distanced them from their fellow-parishioners. This was taken further by their withdrawing from services in their own parishes and forming distinct congregations of the godly, with people from several parishes. Moreover, as Puritans came to see the Church and its services as irredeemably corrupt, many sought to distance themselves from those who continued to take part in them. Pastors warned their flocks to have as little to do with the ungodly as they possibly could. A godly woman was told that she could make love to her ungodly husband, but only if she did not enjoy it.

The changes in the Church pushed through by Charles and Laud played an important part in bringing about the civil war. For the Puritan minority, such changes showed that it was vital to finish the Reformation, left incomplete under Elizabeth. It also showed that drastic change was needed. As the bishops appointed by Charles (and indeed Charles himself) seemed determined to bring 'popery' into the Church, the only way to save Protestantism was to get rid of bishops, which would greatly reduce the king's power over the Church. But the radicalization of the Puritans, and their growing estrangement from their neighbours, would later help the king to attract support. Anti-Puritanism, already visible under Elizabeth and James I, became stronger as the Puritans became more extreme and, from 1641, exercised an influence within Parliament out of all proportion to their numbers in the nation at large.

In the 1630s, however, there were relatively few open signs of discontent in England. People claimed that they were over-rated for ship money, but after the Hampden case it was clear that refusal to pay was not an option. The victims of the king's fiscal devices and fen drainage schemes saw little prospect of redress, other than rioting, for which they would be punished. The law (as interpreted by the courts) was on the king's side, and the English were a law-abiding people. They had become accustomed to dealing with their kings through Parliament, but Charles did without Parliament for eleven years and there was no way of forcing him to call one. The English grumbled and waited for providence to rescue them. Surprisingly, it did so.

Relief came from the north. Scotland was an entirely separate kingdom from England. It had its own king, its own Parliament, its own Church and its own law. The Scots had developed their sense of nationhood out of centuries of wars against England, often conducted with extreme brutality. Relations had improved markedly under Elizabeth, as the English government supported the nascent Protestant movement in Scotland; then James VI of Scotland became James I of England. The level of cross-border violence fell, but centuries of mutual animosity could not be dispelled overnight. As king of both kingdoms, James hoped to carry through a political union, but was rebuffed by the English Parliament. The English expressed contempt for the Scots as grasping, verminous and poor. Scotland had nothing to offer the English, so union could end only with wealth flowing from England to Scotland. The Scots (not least James himself) resented English affectations of superiority, but the Scottish clergy also looked askance at the Church of England. The General Assembly of the Church of Scotland claimed to be the supreme authority in spiritual matters. It accepted that the king was supreme in temporal affairs, but then argued that, as one should obey God before man, in any issue with a spiritual dimension, the king should accept the guidance of the Kirk. As James remarked, it was difficult to see any difference between these claims and those of the papacy.

James VI was a shrewd and pragmatic king. He knew he could not tackle the Kirk head on, so set out to establish his authority over it gradually. He began to appoint bishops, while stressing that these were not 'prelates' on the English model and that they would have to consult with the synods in their dioceses. He established that he had the power to summon the General Assembly, and then did not do so after 1618. He laid down that certain ceremonies similar to those used in England (including the celebration of Christmas) were permissible, but not compulsory. But the Kirk continued to function as before at the parish level, and James did not challenge the principle of Presbyterian church government.

Charles lacked his father's common sense or willingness to confine himself to the possible. Although he was born in Scotland, and retained a Scottish accent, he thought of himself as English and took it for granted that England was superior to Scotland. He did not come to Scotland to be crowned until 1633, eight years after his accession, and then expressed displeasure at the plain form of service used in St Giles' Cathedral in Edinburgh. Convinced of the superiority of the Church of England, he set out to bring the established churches of his three kingdoms into line. The Church of Ireland was governed by bishops, and Charles looked to them to establish Laudian standards of worship. Scotland was a tougher problem. Charles assumed that he was supreme head of the Church of Scotland – which legally he was not – and that he could therefore reform it. Laud and some Scottish bishops drew up a new Prayer Book for Scotland. Few of the Scottish nobility were consulted, which added to their sense that Charles had no interest in Scottish views. They had already been made anxious and angry by an Act of the Scottish Parliament making it possible to claw back earlier royal grants of land, which threatened the landed holdings of many. The introduction of the Prayer Book created a nationwide furore. There were riots in Edinburgh and elsewhere; at Brechin the bishop was able to read from the book without interruption, but only because he had taken the precaution of carrying two loaded pistols into the pulpit. All ranks of society united in condemning the book, anathema as both English and 'popish'.

Charles was not used to such defiance and responded angrily that he expected to be obeyed. The Scottish response was the National Covenant and the reaffirmation of the confession of faith of 1580. All adult males were required to subscribe to the Covenant, which condemned the ceremonies of the Prayer Book. Not all did so willingly, but the early months of 1638 saw much the greater part of the Scottish nation rally in defence of the Kirk and of Presbyterianism. The Covenanters quickly came to dominate Scotland. Charles decided that the only way to reassert his authority was by force. In 1639 he mobilized the English militia, but did not call Parliament. Having gathered together an army, he decided not to invade Scotland and tried conciliation instead. He summoned the Scottish Parliament and the General Assembly and began negotiations. The Covenanters were not eager to fight. They were well aware that England was a much wealthier and more populous kingdom, and believed that they could secure their church only with help from within England, so they emphasized the common ground between the opponents (or victims) of Laudianism on both sides of the border, and called for the summoning of a Parliament in England. The General Assembly, meanwhile, declared that episcopacy was abolished in Scotland. The Scots stressed that their quarrel was not with the English, but with the 'Canterburian faction'. The negotiations produced the Pacification of Berwick, which seemed to give the Scots much of what they wanted. It soon became apparent, however, that Charles interpreted the Pacification very differently from the Covenanters: the Scots were the first to discover that it was very difficult to get Charles to abide by any concessions that he had made. Stung, the Scots Parliament in 1640 passed a Triennial Act, requiring that it should be summoned at least once every three years, and abolished the Lords of the Articles, a committee, nominated by the king, which drew up bills to be considered by the Parliament; without it, the king lost much of his influence there. Meanwhile, both Parliament and the General Assembly appointed committees to deal with any matters arising while they were not in session – in effect, executive bodies independent of the king or the Scottish privy council. By the summer of 1640, Charles had effectively no power in Scotland.

Charles could not ignore such challenges to his authority. He began to mobilize another army and summoned the English

Parliament. He tried to play on traditional English hostility towards the Scots, but was alarmed to discover that some MPs were eager for him to come to terms with the Covenanters. Charles called the Parliament to get money. The Commons were willing to consider this, but also wished to exploit the opportunity that the king's predicament gave them: any grant of money would have a price attached, probably the abandonment of ship money. Charles would not agree, and dissolved Parliament. The abortive 'Short Parliament' of 1640 made his position worse: he had gained nothing and had shown again that he was unwilling to put any trust in his subjects. He had also raised hopes of redress and reconciliation; when those hopes were dashed, there was widespread bitterness and resentment. Laud was widely blamed for the king's intransigence and his London home, Lambeth Palace, was besieged by angry citizens.

With the king's loss of control in Scotland increasingly apparent, his English subjects became bolder. Most had hitherto paid ship money, but now many refused, and the failure of the Short Parliament meant that there was no money to pay the soldiers who were being gathered to fight the Scots. These soldiers were even less tractable than in the previous year. In 1639 many had been mutinous and had expressed their dissatisfaction by pulling down altar rails, smashing stained-glass windows and destroying hedges around enclosed common land. In 1640 it was even more difficult to find recruits, and many of those enlisted were petty criminals or other undesirables, who were undisciplined and riotous; with weapons in their hands they were more likely to plunder civilians and vandalize churches than to obey their officers. Soldiers acted as if they were outside the law, instruments of justice against those they saw as the enemies of the people, especially Catholics and Laudian clergymen. Desertion was rife, the soldiers were truculent and their officers afraid of them, with good reason. A number of officers (especially Catholics) were attacked by their men and at least four were killed.[2] Nor did the soldiers have any sense that, in serving the king, they were fighting for a righteous cause. On the contrary, Scottish propaganda stressed the common ground between the Scots and the aggrieved English; Puritan preachers took up the theme, adding (as the Scots did) that the only way to eradicate popery inside the English Church was to abolish episcopacy 'root and branch'. In August Scottish forces crossed the border. Charles's army was roundly defeated at Newburn and the Scots occupied Northumberland and Durham, and seized Newcastle, on which London depended for its coal.

Newburn was not a major battle, but it was a humiliation. Charles expressed optimism about his prospects of continuing the fight, but his privy council did not, advising him that the only way to prevent the destruction of his authority in Scotland was to agree to the abolition of episcopacy there. Some told him that he had no choice but to call Parliament. Exasperated, Charles summoned an assembly of peers, calling on them to come to the aid of their king with as many men as they could muster. Twelve peers brought with them a petition demanding (not requesting) that the king summon Parliament. Further peers added their signatures and there were a number of supporting petitions, including one from London. Of those who turned up at the meeting – a surprising number claimed to be sick – most told him brusquely that he could not fight, because his army had no enthusiasm for the cause and he had no money to pay them: a request to the City of London for a loan had been rebuffed. When the peers finally assembled, Charles announced his intention to call a Parliament. While not abandoning hope of resuming the war, he opened negotiations with the Scots. He had to choose negotiators acceptable to the Scots: eleven of the sixteen treaty commissioners (who were to serve as long as the negotiations lasted, which was in fact until the summer of 1641) were peers who had signed the recent petition. The future relationship between England and Scotland was in their hands, not the king's.

Charles's defeat in the 'Bishops' Wars' (for that was how it was seen) was humiliating. In his eyes, he had been temporarily worsted by 'rebels' and was now unable to fight to redeem his honour and authority. His plight showed how isolated he had become within England. For probably the first time in history, the English had welcomed a Scottish army as liberators. The Scots, while jubilant, were well aware that they had caught the king in a position of exceptional weakness. To secure themselves and their Kirk against the king in future, they needed to reduce his power within England. The only way to curb the king's power was through the English Parliament. Having occupied the north-east, the Scots demanded that the king pay £850 a day for their subsistence. The only way the king could secure that sort of money was from Parliament. Earlier in the year, when the Short Parliament had not granted him the money he expected, Charles had dissolved it. Now he no longer had that option. The Scots made it clear that if their subsistence was not paid they would march south, and the king would have no way of stopping them. Once Parliament met, it could attach what conditions it wished to its grants of money. The king's commissioners naturally worked closely with the Scots: their task, after all, was to negotiate with them, and their power, as much as Parliament's, depended on the military power of the Scottish army.

In November 1640, at the start of what was to become known as the Long Parliament, MPs came up to London, with eleven years and more of accumulated grievances, but the Scots had their agenda too. To secure themselves, they needed to ensure that Charles would no longer have the power to assert his authority in Scotland by force, or to make innovations within the Church of Scotland. To this end they insisted that the English Parliament should endorse any agreement with the king. They demanded that the two kingdoms should not make war on one another without the consent of their respective Parliaments, and called for a common confession of faith for the two churches; the Scots commissioners and clergy in London also agitated vigorously for the abolition of episcopacy in England. The thinking behind this was clear: to save the Scottish Church from being brought into line with that of England it was necessary to make the English Church like that of Scotland. Thus while many English MPs were concerned primarily to undo what they saw as innovations (by abolishing ship money, for example), the Scots and some of their English allies had a more radical agenda. Moreover, having asserted itself earlier, the Scots Parliament also offered models to follow: for example, the Act to secure triennial Parliaments and the appointment of committees to sit when Parliament was not in session. Within the new Parliament there were to be tensions between those concerned purely with reversing innovations and those who, out of principle or perceived necessity, wished to impose major new restrictions on the power of the crown.

3

STRAFFORD

The Parliament that assembled on 3 November 1640 was to continue, with many vicissitudes and changes of membership, until 1653; revived in 1659 it was finally dissolved in March 1660. It rapidly became the focus of many fears and aspirations. Until the 1620s parliamentary elections had been often rather dull; most constituencies had two members, who were selected following negotiations between a variety of local interests. Contests were avoided, as costly and divisive, so the electors were given no choice but to endorse the nominees of their 'betters'. In the 1620s, contests became more common and some candidates campaigned on political issues. Those who had already sat in Parliament defended their record. Although Parliament's proceedings were supposedly secret, and royal press censorship prevented political news from appearing in print, a great deal of information about debates and issues found its way into the public domain, via manuscript newsletters, correspondence and word of mouth. Contests were even more frequent in the two general elections of 1640, especially the second, and political issues were even more prominent. Opponents of the king's recent policies appealed to the electorate and in many constituencies candidates associated with the court were rejected. It seems probable that, because it was elected at a time when the court was exceptionally unpopular, this House of Commons was 'more puritan in its composition than the country itself'.[1] No previous Parliament had assembled with this measure of public awareness or expectation, and many MPs tried to sustain that awareness, cultivating an image as 'patriots' and printing speeches that they had given – or wished they had given. Those who felt aggrieved by the king's policies, and especially his religious innovations, petitioned Parliament. The committee for scandalous ministers, set up to investigate the misdeeds of the Laudian clergy, received no fewer than 900 petitions.[2] The process of drafting petitions and soliciting subscriptions increased public awareness of contentious issues. Perhaps the most striking difference between the 1620s and the 1640s, indeed, was the role of print. Hitherto the crown had managed to hinder the publication of politically controversial works, but in the confused conditions of 1640 royal censorship of the press proved unenforceable, and so during 1640 there was a veritable explosion of printed news; newsbooks and newspapers began to appear in the autumn of 1641. The news was often accompanied by comment, some serious, some satirical; by the mid-1640s some political journalism revealed an analytical sophistication not seen again until the nineteenth century, or later. The promoters of many of the hundreds of petitions presented to Parliament printed them, which encouraged others to petition and do the same. Initially the king and his supporters deplored the licence of the press and the exposing of the inner secrets of Parliament and the court to public scrutiny and discussion. The leaders of the two Houses, by contrast, soon appreciated the power of the press and fed, but also tried to channel and exploit, the public's hunger for news.

The meeting of the Long Parliament aroused expectations that wrongs of all kinds would now be righted. Often those who felt aggrieved decided to secure redress without waiting for Parliament. Soldiers continued to play a conspicuous role. The king's army remained in being after Newburn: indeed, it was not disbanded until September 1641. He continued to hope that he could use it to wreak revenge on the Covenanters – or re-establish his authority in England. It was quartered in Yorkshire, where it imposed a very heavy burden on the civilian population, partly because of its more or less legitimate demands for quarters and subsistence, partly because of its plunder and violence. The soldiers were paid, but inadequately and in arrears, and they became bored, frustrated and disaffected. They were, it is true, kept together in substantial bodies for months at a time, which made it possible to engage in some serious training, but they were also inclined to take the lead in self-help and the righting of perceived wrongs.[3] Where landlords had enclosed common grazing land for their own use, fences were torn down and (in a few cases) manorial records burned. Crowds raided private deer parks and killed the deer. In the fens of eastern England and the forests of the southwest, the king and those empowered by him had played a leading part in attacks on common rights: now the commoners had their revenge. In London a crowd raided St Paul's, attacked altar rails and destroyed the records of the hated court of high commission; some of the cathedral clergy were assaulted. In many parishes altar rails were pulled down, and images smashed, especially after they were publicly condemned by the House of Commons. Some rioters claimed to be doing Parliament's bidding, others that there was now no law. Widespread reporting of riots in the press encouraged copycat disturbances elsewhere.

The leaders of the two Houses soon realized that popular anger and violence constituted a potent force, which could be used to put pressure on the king. He was so afraid of the people of his capital that he strengthened the fortifications of the Tower of London and did what he could to fortify his sprawling palace at Whitehall. The state opening of Parliament was cancelled. The petitioning peers, many of whom were also commissioners for the Scottish treaty, worked closely with some leading members of the Commons. One of the most prominent of these, John Pym, took the lead in explaining the grievances of recent years in terms of a popish plot. This brought together 'popish' innovations in the Church with an alleged design to establish absolute monarchy, which in the eyes of many Protestants was synonymous with popery; the leading absolute monarchies on the Continent were Spain and France, both Catholic. There can be little doubt that Pym fervently believed in his popish plot, but there is no doubt either that anti-popery was a formidable weapon: at once flexible and malleable, able to accommodate elements which had nothing directly to do with Catholicism, but also deeply divisive. Between Protestantism and Catholicism, Christ or Antichrist, there could be no compromise, no middle way. Moreover, although Charles was not a Catholic, his wife was. There were also numerous Catholics and crypto-Catholics at court; Charles had re-established diplomatic contacts with the Vatican; he had repeatedly offered a variety of concessions to Catholics in Ireland, in return for money; and in 1639 he had successfully appealed to the English Catholics to subscribe money to assist the conquest of Scotland and had issued commissions to leading Catholics (notably the earl of Worcester) to raise troops. Under Elizabeth and James, the Catholics were seen as enemies of the English Protestant monarchy. In 1640–2 only one of many alleged popish plots was directed against the king; the rest were against Parliament or Protestants.[4]

Some of the leaders of both Houses had especial need to cultivate popular support. They had been in touch with the Scots and had encouraged their invasion, in the hope that the Scots could force the king to call a Parliament; legally this was treason – inciting rebellion against the king.[5] The king had had some suspicion of what they were up to and several had their London homes searched in May 1640. These dissidents blamed the misgovernment of the 1630s on evil counsellors. As some had been privy councillors, or had close links with people at court, this claim was based partly on inside knowledge. The peers among them claimed that, during failures of royal government, the peerage had the duty and the authority to take the lead in putting matters right. This view was to some extent shared by their allies in the Commons, who were linked to them by ties of clientage, friendship and shared godliness. In the Lords the key figures in late 1640 were the earls of Bedford and Warwick; each had a network of supporters in both Houses. Another much respected figure was the earl of Essex, and there were others such as the earls of Northumberland, Holland and Hertford who had held high office in the 1630s, including commands in the armies raised in 1639–40.

In each House there emerged a group sufficiently distinct and identifiable to be given the nickname of a 'Junto'. In the Lords Warwick came to be the central figure in the oppositionist Junto; in the Commons a key figure – but not the only one – was Pym. Both peers and MPs shared with the Scots a need to reduce the king's power to a point where he was no longer able to harm them. Many were also committed to the abolition of episcopacy 'root and branch', either because they sincerely believed it was necessary, or (more likely) because they knew that the Scots expected it, and they needed to keep the Scots' goodwill. But many, probably the majority, of MPs had no such radical agenda. They wished to reverse innovations and root out abuses in Church and State, but not to change fundamentally the nature of the monarchy or the constitution. They claimed, and may truly have believed, that the king was basically well-meaning, but had been misled. One aspect of the redress of grievances, therefore, was the removal of evil counsellors. Several leading figures in the Personal Rule went abroad and others, including Laud, were impeached. But impeachment was a legal process. The Lords, who heard such cases, expected proper standards of proof, but that was not always possible: as one MP remarked, evil counsel was not given in public assemblies but whispered in corners. This became clear in the case of Thomas Wentworth, earl of Strafford.

The Commons began to collect evidence against Strafford a week after Parliament first met, and he became the main focus of its proceedings over the next six months. In one sense he was an odd choice. He had been away from London for most of the 1630s, first in the North and then in Ireland. He was less universally hated than Laud, who was impeached in December 1640 (though not tried until 1644). What distinguished Strafford was his ruthlessness. The king's other advisers were adept at finding legal subterfuges for raising money; Strafford dealt in violence. Those who fell foul of him in Ireland found themselves imprisoned without trial, as he bullied and browbeat opponents into submission. He managed to unite almost all sections of Irish society, Protestant and Catholic, Irish, English and Scots, against him as he advanced the king's interests, increasing the royal revenue, and building himself a large fortune in the process. When the king faced problems in Scotland, and his English ministers urged negotiation or compromise, Strafford alone urged him to rely on force. In 1639 he came over to England to head the war effort. He allegedly told the king that he was 'loose and absolved from all rules of government'. 'Being reduced to extreme necessity, he was to do everything that power might admit.'[6] Admittedly, this story rested on the single testimony of Sir Henry Vane the elder, who 'remembered' the words only during his third interrogation by the Commons; other privy councillors said that there was no truth in it. (If it was true, the words no doubt gave a delightful frisson to the king, who was a far from forceful character and tended to be swept along by stronger personalities.) Strafford urged him to bring over a newly raised Irish army, mostly Catholic, which he could use to reduce 'this kingdom'. This army remained in being, under Strafford's notional command, until the summer of 1641, a disruptive presence in Ulster and a possible threat to the English Parliament. For those who had encouraged the Scots, Strafford was dangerous in a way other ministers were not. He planned to accuse leading MPs of treasonable dealings with the Scots. At the same time the king would 'review' the garrison of the recently strengthened Tower, to have soldiers ready if need arose. The news leaked out and the plan was aborted, or postponed, but the incident confirmed what some peers and MPs already knew. The Lords' decision to place Strafford in custody reduced the danger that he could personally use military force against them; but unease remained. They needed to destroy Strafford before he destroyed them.

Strafford was charged with treason. Under existing law, treason was defined in terms of taking up arms against the king or conspiring against him. From the outset, Pym argued that the definition should be extended. Strafford, he argued, had advised the king to misuse his powers so extensively that he had alienated his people to a point where his safety was seriously threatened. In response to the practice of James I and Charles I of stretching the letter of the law at the expense of its spirit, lawyers and politicians had sought to identify and articulate the basic principles underlying the common law and the unwritten 'ancient constitution'. They began to use the phrase 'fundamental laws' to describe these principles. The problem was that there was no consensus about what these fundamental laws were. When one MP asked about this, during the debates on Strafford, there was an embarrassed silence before he was told that, if he did not know, he should not be sitting in Parliament.[7] Pym's definition of treason was superficially plausible, but could mean in practice that 'treason' became giving the king advice which Parliament disliked. In Pym's words 'to endeavour the subversion of the laws of this kingdom was treason of the highest nature' – and he assumed that the Commons were competent to state what those laws were.[8] Ultimately, however, the case against Strafford lay not in legal argument but in the charge that he intended to bring over the 'Irish popish army'. Strafford agreed that this was true, though argued that the army was to be used against the Scottish rebels, not against the English. He denied telling the king that he was 'loose and absolved from all rules of government', although Vane (and his son, who had seen the notes his father had taken before destroying key documents at the king's command) insisted that he had indeed done so.

Some peers eagerly promoted the impeachment. They included several who had been close to the king in the late 1630s, and whose hostility to Strafford was based on personal knowledge that they could not make public, for fear of damaging the king. (It has been remarked that those who trusted Charles I least were often those who knew him best.) Others supported the impeachment because they feared punishment for their dealings with the Scots. But the majority in the Lords took their judicial responsibilities seriously. Strafford argued his case forcefully and with great determination and wit, despite poor health and efforts by the Commons to hinder him; the impeachment proceedings were faltering well before they collapsed in confusion on 10 April 1641. Hardliners in the Commons had become frustrated by the Lords' concern to follow due process and their agreeing to adjournments for the accused to consult counsel and send to Ireland for documents. As relations between the Houses became strained, the Commons resolved to bring in a bill of attainder. This stated that Strafford was guilty of treason and should suffer the appropriate punishments. Such bills had often been passed after unsuccessful rebellions, when there was no doubting the guilt of the defeated rebels. There was no such certainty in this case: indeed, the gradual abandonment of the impeachment showed the weakness of the Commons' case. There was stiff opposition to the attainder bill in the Commons; some argued that it amounted to judicial murder, and many absented themselves when it came to the final vote. Nevertheless, the bill passed the Commons on 21 April by 204 votes to 59, and was sent up to the Lords.

The king had taken steps to defuse the hostility to Strafford. He had given his assent, albeit with bad grace, to a bill for triennial Parliaments: MPs of just about all shades of opinion agreed that guaranteed regular Parliaments were essential to prevent another period of 'personal rule' such as that in the 1630s. At times the king seemed conciliatory. He declared that he would rule within the law and collect only those revenues which were legal. He would return the Church to the condition it had been in under Elizabeth and James I. He appointed several of the petitioning peers to the privy council, including the earls of Bedford, Hertford and Essex – but not the most implacable and influential of all, Warwick. Here, perhaps, was a sign that he wished to receive better 'counsel' – except that he did not call the privy council regularly and showed little inclination to take its advice. Perhaps because it was now a politically more mixed body, the council tended to confine itself to minor and routine business. Meanwhile, much of the legal basis of the Personal Rule was gradually unpicked by the committee of petitions in the Lords, who used their authority as the supreme court of law to declare various royal practices and actions illegal.

The king's appointment of petitioning peers to offices and as privy councillors could be seen as an attempt to become reconciled to his critics, but these 'bridge' appointments were only one side of a possible deal. In return Pym and some of his allies proposed a modernization of the king's revenues, providing enough money to fund the government, without recourse to the contentious fiscal expedients of the past fifteen years. But most backbench MPs were interested first and foremost in promoting the interests of their localities and redressing local grievances. Until that was done they had no intention of voting more than the absolute minimum of revenue, and blamed royal shortages of money on incompetence and embezzlement. As a result so much business was brought into the Commons that the House could not decide what to consider first, and money bills became lost in the general mass of bills and business.[9] This did not necessarily perturb the likes of Pym and Warwick. The key to power over the king lay not in the passing of legislation, or the judicial decisions of the Lords' committee of petitions, but in control of the revenue. If for the moment the king was desperately short of money, he could not get rid of Parliament and could be pressured into making concessions. Holding out the prospect of a more substantial revenue in future might have a similar effect.

If at times Charles seemed determined to be conciliatory, and to have learned from his mistakes, at others he did not. Faced with a choice between conciliation and threat, he generally pursued both options, in the naive hope that threats could make his subjects more inclined to submit to him. He harboured hopes of reasserting himself by force. On 14 April a request from the Commons that he disband the Irish army was met with a blank refusal. Charles may have hoped that the planned marriage between his daughter Mary and William, the son of Frederick Henry, prince of Orange, would be followed by Dutch military aid. The queen certainly did, and dabbled in wilder schemes, soliciting help from the pope and the French. But the pope would do nothing unless Charles formally converted to Catholicism, a complete impossibility in the current political circumstances. Cardinal Richelieu, Louis XIII's chief minister, preferred to establish good relations with Parliament. When the queen talked of going to France, allegedly for her health, Richelieu made it clear that the king would refuse to receive her.

Meanwhile, the English army was sitting glumly in the North, complaining about its arrears of pay, some of which had been diverted to the Scots; some said they were ready to fight the Scots, if Parliament so wished. From this situation emerged the 'army plot'. This consisted of a disparate group of (often muddled) intrigues. A group of officers, including some MPs, had drawn up a petition to Parliament, hoping it would lead to their securing their pay and some of the king's prerogatives, but also to the king making concessions to Parliament. There had been meetings of officers calling for changes in the high command and talk of bringing the army south and securing the Tower. One of the officers, George Goring, betrayed their plans to some of the peers and to Pym. The plan to bring the army to London was abandoned: the soldiers were resentful that Parliament had failed to provide their pay, but not to the extent of threatening to use force against Parliament. The plan to secure the Tower continued. This was master-minded (if that is the right word) by a courtier, soldier and poet called Sir John Suckling, who aimed to raise a small force on the pretext of going to serve the king of Portugal, who was in rebellion against Spain, and to lodge them in the Tower. The lieutenant of the Tower was suspicious and refused to admit the men. The gathering of even a modest force of one hundred men attracted the attention of nervous Londoners, who watched the gates of the Tower in their hundreds and peti-tioned the Lords to ask the king to withdraw the men. The king answered that the soldiers were needed to secure the munitions in the Tower, especially in view of the great crowds gathering around it. The Lords responded by sending Lord Newport to take command of the Tower; they informed the king, who appointed him as constable. The Lords further ordered 500 of the Tower Hamlets militia to be stationed in the Tower.[10] There were also plans to send some units of the army to secure Portsmouth, where Goring was the governor, and the queen hoped to land troops from France. When these schemes leaked out, some of the officers involved fell over themselves to testify to Parliament; others, closely associated with the queen, fled abroad. But the various intrigues had never been entirely secret. There had been frequent rumours of army plotting since Goring had made his revelations at the end of March, and Charles showed no obvious displeasure towards those who had confessed their involvement. It seems that he was not unhappy that those whom he saw as his enemies should see the army as a threat, or believe half-baked schemes had been more dangerous than they really were.[11]

Even if Pym had been able to deliver on his financial assur-ances, it is unlikely that Charles really wanted a deal. He made it absolutely clear that he had no intention of dismissing Strafford, even though the earl more than once begged him to do so.[12] For Charles it was a matter of honour. He attended the Lords formally on the day Strafford delivered his answer to the charges against him, whereupon the Lords resolved that all proceedings while he was in the House were null and void. During the trial proper, the king attended, but sat in an alcove, supposedly incognito, while his throne remained prominent and vacant. The king's obduracy made his opponents all the more determined to destroy Strafford: they believed that they needed him dead in order to demonstrate the king's weakness and 'reduce the king to a necessity of granting'.[13] They also appealed to the wider public. The trial attracted huge public interest: there was room in Westminster Hall for over a thousand spectators, as well as the two Houses. The Commons' passing the attainder bill increased the political temperature. The king eventually accepted that he would have to dismiss Strafford from his service, but assured him 'upon the word of a king, you shall not suffer in life, honour or fortune'.[14] The majority of the Lords initially thought that the bill was unjust and also an affront to their jurisdiction. The Commons leaders set out to put pressure on the Lords and on the king to agree to Strafford's execution. A petition for 'justice' against Strafford was presented to the Commons on 24 April, allegedly with twenty thousand signatures. On 28 April news broke of a plan for Strafford to escape abroad. Rumours abounded of popish and army plots and possible military coups. On the 29th Oliver St John, the newly appointed solicitor general, put to the Lords the Commons' case for the attainder bill. After rehearsing arguments from statute and precedent, he based his case on necessity: Strafford's plan to bring over the Irish army posed such a dire threat to English liberties and religion that extreme measures were not only justified but essential. Using a metaphor that would strike a chord with the peers he declared 'it was never accounted either cruelty or foul play to knock foxes and wolves on the head ... because they be beasts of prey'. Lest he had failed to make his point, St John elsewhere referred to Strafford as a mad bull and a mastiff.[15] His speech, detailed and eloquent, had a profound effect on the Lords: many who had been unconvinced by the legal justification for an attainder now began to change their minds.

Public alarm and anger continued to mount. On 1 May the king was persuaded to address the Houses to plead for Strafford's life, but lost any credit he might have gained by a haughty reference to his conscience. The Commons again pressed him to disband the Irish army; again he refused, saying he would disband it only when the English and Scots armies in the North had been disbanded. Suckling's plan to install soldiers in the Tower was meant to have been carried out on 2 May and was thwarted by the actions of the citizens and the Lords on 3 May. On that day, as the peers arrived to debate the attainder bill, their House was surrounded by angry crowds, calling for 'justice' against Strafford. The names of the 'Straffordians', the fifty-nine MPs who had voted against the bill, were posted up amid general execration. Meanwhile, in the Commons, concern was expressed about the mood of the army in the North, and it was resolved to send a letter assuring the soldiers that they would receive their pay. Pym stressed the need for unity. The king needed to be shown, he said, how much he had been misled by evil counsellors. He brought forward a 'Protestation', on which he claimed all good Protestants could agree; it was to be subscribed by all members of Parliament. It set out allegations of a popish plot to establish 'an arbitrary and tyrannical government'; there were references to illegal taxation and superstitious innovations in the Church. Those who subscribed promised to defend Parliament, the Protestant religion, the doctrine (but not the discipline) of the Church of England and the king's 'royal person, honour and estate' against the papists. (There was no reference to the king's powers or prerogatives.) As one of Pym's allies put it: '[we] may all swear to be true to our king and defend our church and commonwealth'.[16] After MPs the citizens and clergy of London were invited to subscribe, and their example was followed by many others elsewhere. When a bill was brought in requiring all adult males to take it, it was printed with a polemical preamble about the danger from plots and popery.

The Protestation spread alarm at the popish threat from Westminster into the provinces, and with it the idea that active resistance to authority could be legitimate; the fact that it was subscribed by MPs in the first instance gave it a considerable measure of authority. The very business of drawing up a declaration which people were asked to subscribe as a measure of their Protestant credentials – 'a mark by which they might know who were good men, lovers of their country' – was deeply divisive.[17] The sense of crisis was soon ratcheted up even further, as details emerged of the army plot. The preamble to the printed Protestation declared that there had been great endeavours 'to bring the English army into a misunderstanding of this Parliament, thereby to incline that army with force to bring to pass those wicked counsels'.[18] Similarly, when the close (or secret) committee set up to investigate the plot reported on 8 June, they presented their evidence in such a way as to suggest that the plot had been more coherent, and more popish, than it really was.[19] As more and more details became public, it looked clear that the roots of the plot lay in Whitehall, with the king and queen. Fear of violence and popish plotting became still more intense, as did popular hostility towards the queen. The mounting anxiety, the revelations of Suckling's plot, and the increasingly threatening behaviour of the London crowds, reinforced the impact of St John's speech and helped change the Lords' attitude to the attainder bill. Some peers stayed away. Others who remained protested that they could not debate freely when their House was surrounded by intimidating crowds. But all the Protestant peers subscribed the Protestation and the attainder bill passed through the House on 8 May, by fifty-one votes to nine.

By now London was in a ferment. There were rumours that papists in the provinces were planning to massacre Protestants, that the French had captured Jersey and Guernsey, and that troops were massing in France for an invasion of England. By 8 May the queen was seriously alarmed and had to be dissuaded by the French ambassador from fleeing to Portsmouth, where she hoped that she would be safe until a French army came to rescue her. It was as well that she did not go, as the Houses had sent a delegation to secure the town; the Houses also resolved to put the kingdom in a posture of defence. Also on the 8th the Houses sent two delegations to urge the king to give his assent to the attainder bill; they were accompanied by large armed crowds, who expressed particular hostility towards the queen. Whitehall was effectively under siege. There were rumours at court that peers and MPs were summoning their supporters from the provinces and fears that the crowds would break into the palace. The queen, her priests and her ladies feared that this would happen and that they would be massacred. They frantically sought out their confessors and prepared for the worst.

Fearing for the safety of his wife and family, Charles's resolution gradually crumbled. On the 9th he summoned his privy council, who to a man advised him to yield. The judges assured him that Strafford was indeed guilty of treason. When he asked the bishops if he could in conscience give his assent to the bill, and in effect condemn Strafford to death, he received mixed advice. After hours of vacillation, he gave in, rather than put his wife's life at risk, and gave his assent to the attainder bill and a bill against the dissolution of this Parliament without its own consent. The next day, after much wriggling, he signed Strafford's death warrant, after the Lords had made it clear that they were prepared to go ahead with the execution without it. He remarked that 'my lord of Strafford's condition is more happy than mine'.[20] He also agreed, reluctantly, that the execution should be public. Two days later a joyful crowd estimated at 200,000 watched Strafford's execution on Tower Hill. He died with exemplary courage, refusing the offer of a blindfold, saying he wished to look his executioner in the face.

In one sense, Strafford's death eased the atmosphere of crisis. Rightly or wrongly, he had come to epitomize the fear of violence and massacre which had built up, especially since the passing of the attainder bill and the revelation of Suckling's plot. He had become a near-universal hate figure. When Charles begged Bedford, Essex and Pym to do whatever they could to save Strafford, Essex replied brusquely: 'Stone dead hath no fellow'.[21] Warwick, too, insisted that Strafford had to die, and with Bedford's death on 9 May Warwick became the dominant figure in the 'Junto' in the Lords. Strafford's death also raised the stakes in the struggle between Charles and his opponents in Parliament. Charles, quite reasonably, saw the destruction of Strafford as murder, a misuse of legislative power compounded by a stirring up of the people to disorder and violence. His anger was no doubt sharpened by a sense of shame at having capitulated and given his assent to the attainder bill, but this made him all the more eager for revenge: this was a blood feud. He had never accepted that he needed to make concessions to Parliament, or anyone else, because he did not believe that he had done anything wrong. Now, urged on by the queen, he was more determined than ever to find some way of getting together an army that could crush his enemies, after which he could reclaim the rightful powers that he had been forced to surrender, and punish the likes of Warwick, Pym and Essex for their crimes. As early as 18 May news leaked out that he planned to go to Scotland, hoping to exploit the growing rifts between the Scots and the English Parliament and within the Covenanter movement.[22] This raised the spectre that the Scots army, the guarantor of Parliament's existence and the ultimate source of the power of the reformist 'Junto', would leave England. The English army in the North and the 'Irish popish' army were still in being and, if the king became reconciled with his enemies in Scotland, there was the still more dangerous possibility that Charles might be able to use the Scottish army as well.

Pym, Essex and their friends were well aware of this. Gossip and speculation were rife at court, and one of the queen's ladies in waiting, Lady Carlisle, kept Pym informed of what was being said in the queen's circle, which was forever forming airy designs to gather together soldiers. Like the Scots, the Junto came to appreciate that the only way to safeguard themselves against royal revenge was to take away the king's power to harm them. Neither the Junto nor the king was interested in negotiation: threats were met with counter-threats, as the spiral of mutual distrust grew ever more serious. Reducing the king's power meant first and foremost his control over the army, but to ensure responsible government it would also be necessary to ensure that he was responsibly advised. The Junto aimed to change not the structure of government but its personnel: if reliable men (like themselves) were appointed to the top posts and the privy council, and the king was made to follow the advice of the council, they believed that all would go well. As he was clearly reluctant to appoint good counsellors voluntarily, Parliament should have the power to approve, or reject, his choice of advisers. It had become clear from the Strafford trial that impeachment was an inadequate way of removing evil counsellors: it could take place only after damage had been done, proof was difficult, and the nature of the treason laws made it hard to secure a conviction. It would be far better, for the safety of the kingdom, if evil counsellors could be prevented from being appointed in the first place. But these proposals were, for many MPs, unacceptably radical. Most MPs believed that the constitution was basically sound, if operated with goodwill and good sense. They expected the king to govern – that was his job – and that to do so effectively he needed the traditional prerogatives of the crown, which included the right to choose his ministers and the right to command the armed forces. A king who lacked these powers was, in seventeenth-century terms, not a king at all. The problem facing the Junto was to persuade these members that the threat to their safety, and that of the Protestant religion, posed by the king and those around him were so severe and immediate as to justify radical changes to the traditional constitution. In doing so, it did not help that it could not reveal some of its information, or where it came from.

For the moment, with Strafford gone and the sense of imminent peril lifted, it was difficult to sustain that feeling of danger. Members of the Junto might be deeply worried by the implications of the king's planned journey to Scotland, but there was no longer the sense of crisis in the streets of London that had been so evident at the beginning of May. Parliament now embarked seriously on a programme of reform, much of it dealing with particular grievances of the 1630s. In part, this involved a process of investigation, gathering information and encouraging petitions, which could be seen as providing Parliament with a mandate for action – and further evidence against evil counsellors. It had already passed the Triennial Act and, at the height of the Strafford crisis, the Act against this Parliament's being dissolved without its own consent. These diminished somewhat the king's prerogative of summoning and dismissing Parliaments at will, but could be seen as leaving the basic substance intact. Charles did not think so: he saw any diminution of his prerogative as a dangerous threat to the monarchy. Nevertheless, he was now required to meet Parliament for only fifty days in every three years, and most of his predecessors had managed to live with Parliaments and in some ways had found them extremely useful. One of the monarchy's greatest assets was the willingness of the English to submit to royal authority and their expectation that the king should govern. Charles was temperamentally incapable of understanding this, or that a quite genuine rhetoric of the obedience of subjects could be combined with a robust insistence that the king should follow the rules laid down by law and, more nebulously, by the 'fundamental laws'. Charles's seemingly wilful incomprehension drove essentially obedient subjects to make demands which they had not made of any of his predecessors. Clear and repeated evidence that he planned to reassert his authority by armed force drove his Parliament and his people to seek to restrict his authority further.

Both the Acts relating to the summoning and dissolution of Parliaments had been passed because they seemed necessary. The first would guarantee regular Parliaments and so maintain dialogue between king and people. The second was a one-off emergency measure, possibly to counter the threat that the king might dissolve Parliament to save Strafford. From June, Acts were passed dealing with many past grievances. Ship money and impositions were declared illegal, as was raising tonnage and poundage without Parliament's consent. Other laws dealt with the royal forests and knighthood fines. These reforms meant that the king was left with few revenues of his own, certainly not enough to support the government. Parliament voted him tonnage and poundage, but only for short periods, so that he would be forced to keep Parliament in being, to renew this grant, or else he would quickly run out of money. This unprecedented power of the purse gave the Long Parliament far greater bargaining power, when dealing with the king, than its predecessors of the 1620s and earlier. This power was shown when Parliament dismantled some of the institutional apparatus of the Personal Rule. The court of Star Chamber was abolished, as was the court of high commission, an ecclesiastical court used to impose Laudian innovations on the Church. All this was relatively uncontentious.

The general sense of consensus perhaps explains the relatively moderate tone of the Ten Propositions, which were approved by the Commons and carried up to the Lords on 24 June. These were not to be presented to the king as a whole, but were proposed as an agenda on which the Houses could agree, and proceed to implement as appropriate, through bills or petitions. Their key concern was national security and the danger from papists and plots. They stressed that the king needed to choose better counsellors, put the army and navy in safe hands, and overhaul the militia; there were calls for the expulsion of the papal nuncio, firmer measures against Catholic recusants, and the removal of Catholics from court. However, instead of suggesting that the king should be made to appoint counsellors acceptable to Parliament, it was merely suggested that the two Houses should petition him to do so and to remove counsellors against whom the Houses might have 'just exceptions' – a considerably more muted wording than had been proposed originally; several MPs vigorously defended the king's right to choose his own counsellors.[23] The Lords made a few amendments to the Propositions, but in general they offered a programme behind which the Houses could unite; the Lords were particularly active in measures to strengthen national defence, but were much less keen on severe measures against Catholic recusants: Catholic peers had the right to sit in the Lords. The Propositions presented the king with an opportunity to re-establish trust and goodwill. He did not take it. He agreed to dismiss the nuncio and to disband the army in the North, once money had been provided to pay it off and the Scots had gone home; but on the crucial question of counsel, he said simply that he did not know of any evil counsellors.[24]

The one consistently divisive issue was religion. In December 1640 a massive petition had called for abolition of episcopacy, root and branch. When the matter was debated, in February 1641, the Laudians found few defenders, and there was much support for reforming episcopacy, but many were concerned at the implications of abolition. The bishops were not much loved, but episcopacy was a part of the ancient constitution. A bill to abolish episcopacy was debated at length in the Commons. The final text no longer survives, but it is clear that it neither paved the way to establish Scottish-style Presbyterianism, nor opened the way to full religious liberty. Its main concern was to put ecclesiastical jurisdiction and the bulk of church property into the hands of lay commissioners, thus carrying still further the lay (and especially gentry) control of the church that had developed since the Reformation. The church courts, as directed by godly gentlemen, could be used to reform the morals of the people, but would no longer molest godly ministers. The profits of church lands could ease the financial problems of the state and enhance the stipends of the clergy, thus reinforcing the parish system. A synod was to devise a new form of church government. One aim of the bill was undoubtedly to weaken the clergy: the Commons had been extremely annoyed by the Lords' refusal to exclude the bishops from their House.[25] The Junto – especially the peers negotiating the treaty with the Scots – promoted the bill because they knew the Scots expected bishops to be abolished and they were eager to maintain the goodwill of their Scottish allies. But they were in no hurry, and once the Scottish treaty (which contained no explicit commitment to root and branch) had been accepted by the Scottish Parliament, on 3 August, interest in the bill disappeared and it was quietly dropped.[26] There was no chance that it could have passed the Lords, especially while there were bishops in the Upper House. (The Lords did agree to exclude clergyman from exercising any civil authority). Moreover, the attack on episcopacy seemed part of a wider assault on Prayer Book Anglicanism. In January 1641 there was a proposal in the Commons to order the removal of altars and rails and the destruction of 'superstitious' church furniture and images, and the House later refused to issue an order condemning those who failed to use the Prayer Book. The Lords, more moderately, ordered in March that the communion table should 'stand decently in the ancient place where it ought to do by the law' and as it had for the past sixty years.[27] The Commons' order to cleanse church interiors of 'superstitious' items was finally agreed on 8 September, in a thin House. The Lords responded by publishing an earlier order that divine service should be performed 'as it is appointed by the Acts of Parliament'.[28]

The Commons' order, the work of one House of Parliament, in a matter over which it had no jurisdiction, had no legal force. It was published by the Commons with a statement that the Lords had rejected it by a very narrow margin. This was part of a pattern which went back to at least December 1640, when the Commons' committee for scandalous ministers invited parishioners, in print, to make complaints against the clergy. On the basis of these complaints ministers were harassed, summoned to London and interrogated; some were kept waiting for weeks by the committee and put to considerable expense. Now the Commons' order was seen by Puritan zealots as authorizing the 'cleansing' of church interiors. Some claimed that the Protestation bound people to abolish not only the government and discipline of the Church, but also its liturgy and cere-monies. Many clergymen now stopped using the Prayer Book and wearing the surplice, the white gown which they had been required to wear hitherto. Laudian clergymen were abused, services were disrupted, prayer books and surplices were torn and defiled. The Commons also authorized 'godly' parish-ioners to invite 'godly' lecturers to preach in their church, where the existing minister did not provide lectures, additional sermons on top of the normal round of services. Sometimes the newcomers were welcomed, but often they were not. In many cases a 'godly' minority used the authority of the Commons to impose their wishes, and their form of service, on the majority. In some cases, parishioners locked the church doors and refused to allow the new preacher in.

Laudian clergymen clung to their parishes and ignored Parliament's orders, but those who opposed the Commons' drive for godly reformation were by no means only Laudians. Many who had disliked Laudianism resented this vandalizing of their churches – some even defended altar rails – and being deprived of their familiar services and rituals. Whereas hitherto most petitions to Parliament about religion had called for the eradication of popish superstition, in the second half of 1641 there was a growing number in favour of the Prayer Book. According to a petition from Huntingdonshire in 1642, godly minorities demanded that 'what they dislike must not only to themselves but to all others be scandalous and burdensome and must be cried out upon as great and unsupportable griev-ances'.[29] Meanwhile, particularly in London, some were opting out of the parish system altogether. Taking the separation of the godly from the ungodly one stage further than gadding to sermons, godly preachers formed their own independent congregations, worshipping as they thought fit; some had laymen as their preachers. They rejected not only episcopacy but any established church, or indeed any church that mixed saints and sinners. A true church, they claimed, was a voluntary association of 'visible saints'. One indication of the alarm felt by Londoners at these developments was the election of a conservative lord mayor, Sir Richard Gurney, on 28 September.

Some detected in the attack on bishops a more general threat to hierarchy and authority. As one MP remarked, if they came to 'parity' (equality) in the Church, this might lead to 'parity' in society at large; the bishops had a constitutional right to sit in the Lords.[30] This anxiety was strengthened by the appearance of independent gathered churches. Members of the social elite in the seventeenth century often expressed alarm at the fragility of the forces of order. With no standing army and no police force, law and order depended on constables, watchmen and the militia, all drawn from the social groups that they were supposed to be policing. When looking at early modern riots, particularly those protesting against enclosures and high food prices, one is generally struck by the discipline and restraint of the rioters, their limited use of violence and their profound sense of legitimation. But the rioting in 1640–2 was different: it was considerably more violent and was often political and religious in nature. Contemporaries habitually spoke of the people as beasts, driven by their lusts, who (if they only knew their strength) would rise up and slaughter and plunder the wealthy. If they did not do so, it was because they feared the exemplary punishments of the law or had been indoctrinated by the Church to know their place; but now they seemed to have lost all respect for the law.[31] Moreover, some were now opting out of the Church, which no longer had any influence over them. In so doing, they threatened a 'breach of that union which is the sacred band and preservation of the common peace of church and state'.[32]

In 1641 the people seemed to be becoming aware of their strength. They were taking the law into their own hands, and were getting away with it. Most worrying, there were those at Westminster who seemed to encourage them to do so, notably through the Protestation. Much of the violence was against those identified by the Commons as enemies of Parliament and the Protestant nation: Catholics, Laudians and courtiers (or 'cavaliers'). In Colchester there was sustained violence against Sir John Lucas, an unpopular landlord, a vocal supporter of the court and a promoter of Laudianism. In August 1642 the violence spilled into the countryside, as crowds from Colchester and Ipswich marauded along the Stour valley, searching the houses of Royalists and Catholics for weapons; what began as targeted searches degenerated into almost indis-criminate plunder.[33] When the crowd began to pull down the house of Lady Rivers, a Catholic, she appealed to Warwick, who was very popular among the people of Essex, to rescue her. Warwick was away, but his steward set out to find Lady Rivers. He was staggered by the hostility he encountered among the people, many of whom 'behaved themselves as if there had been a dissolution of all government'. Great crowds assembled when he came to Sudbury; some claimed that he was Lord Rivers and he was in some physical danger, until the town clerk assured the people that he was indeed Warwick's steward. Even then there was no prospect of finding Lady Rivers (who had in fact escaped to London). An MP who was believed to have helped her escape had to keep an armed guard in his house, to protect it against the 'rabble'.[34]

By the time of the Stour valley riots, England was on the verge of civil war. In June and July 1641, with Strafford dead, the atmosphere was considerably less fraught – until the time approached for the king's departure to Scotland. At the same time, the Scottish army finally prepared to leave Northumberland and Durham. The king's announcement inevitably provoked speculation, and suspicion about his intentions. Now that he was in financial thrall to the English Parliament, the only way that he could possibly reassert his autonomy was by military force, and this is probably what

Charles hoped to achieve by his journey to Scotland. At the very least he hoped to drive a wedge between his Scottish and English opponents – the Scots commissioners in London had gone home months before. He was soon to show that, in an effort to secure Scottish support, he was prepared to make concessions to the Scots that he was not prepared to make to the English.

Once again Pym's Junto sought to alert the Houses and the wider public to the alarm that they felt. The Lords rejected the bill requiring every adult male to subscribe the Protestation. The Commons declared that the Protestation was designed to identify and root out papists, and resolved that nobody who refused to subscribe was fit to bear office; it ordered that this resolution should be printed and sent into the provinces. A resolution of one House had no authority, but the Commons were beginning to print their 'votes' in a calculated appeal for popular support. They were seriously alarmed at the prospect of the king's going to Scotland. The armies had not been disbanded, the Scots were still in the North, and the programme set out in the Ten Propositions was far from completed. (In fact the Scots had gone by 25 August, but the English army was not fully disbanded until 18 September.) Most crucial of all, the key issue of 'counsel' had not been addressed, and the Commons remained anxious and distrustful, if not of the king, at least of those around him. As a result, when on 10 August the king left for Scotland, the Commons, following the earlier example of the Scottish Parliament, sent a committee to Scotland to keep an eye on him.

Surprisingly, the king had made little provision for government in England in his absence, despite rumours of foreign attack: the regency commission he appointed to take charge of the government was too divided to be effective and its powers were limited and ill defined. It had no power to give the royal assent to bills. The inadequacy of these arrangements drove the Houses to appoint committees to sit and act during the recess. This assumption of executive responsibilities was made more acceptable by the fact that members of the Junto now held most of the great offices of state, particularly those relating to the military and the management of the revenue. In attempting to win them over with grants of office, Charles had handed them great power. After Pym had produced further revelations about the army plot, the Commons resolved to draw up a remonstrance about the state of the nation and appointed a committee to consider who should exercise what power over the militia: somebody had to take responsibility for national security and to counter any possible armed threat from the king. The Lords, as before, were very willing to co-operate with the Commons on matters of defence and security, and were equally concerned that the militia should be in hands acceptable to both Houses; a militia bill was brought in, providing for a sweeping purge of lords lieutenant and deputy lieutenants. Charles had appointed the earl of Essex to command all forces south of the Trent, so that preparations for defence made in conjunction with Essex could be seen as authorized by the king. But the Houses had shown already that they were prepared to take executive action, encroaching on the king's responsibilities, if they saw an overwhelming need to do so. After the revelation of Suckling's plot, they had ordered that the ports should be closed, to stop any miscreants escaping abroad, effectively appointed Newport constable of the Tower, and used the Tower Hamlets militia to secure it.

Now Parliament began to issue 'ordinances' to secure the munitions in the Tower and at Hull, and to send instructions to the committee in Scotland. Most of these ordinances activated existing statutes, but one, while claiming to do so, went further. The ordinance for disarming papists widened the definition of 'recusants' to include men with Catholic children or servants, and those suspected to be 'popishly affected' or dangerous. Such was the alarm about the threat from plots and popery that the ordinance met with little opposition.[35] By default, and with barely an adverse comment, Parliament was beginning to perform the sort of executive tasks which had traditionally been the prerogative of the king. By now members were weary, fearful of plague (which was rife in London), and pining for home. At last, on 9 September, the Houses dispersed for a long overdue recess.

4

THE GRAND REMONSTRANCE

The Parliamentary recess brought to an end ten months of often frenetic activity at Westminster. As the dust settled, MPs and the wider public were able to take stock of the situation. Much had been achieved. The 'evil advisers' of the Personal Rule had been dispersed and imprisoned; Strafford was dead. The fiscal devices that had enabled the king to rule without Parliament had been outlawed, and the institutions that had been used to hound religious and political dissidents had been abolished. The king was now financially dependent on Parliament and so would have to heed its views, and those of his people, in the future. For many, including probably a majority in both Houses, this was enough to put the old constitution back on an even keel and to make the king rule responsibly, without the need for a frontal assault on his essential prerogatives. Others were less optimistic. Warwick, Pym and their allies in both Houses knew that the king would be revenged on them if it was ever in his power to do so. At the moment he seemed to lack that power, but if he could get his hands on a sizeable army the situation would be transformed: unlike Scotland or Ireland, England was not a heavily armed or militarized nation. That was why the king's journey to Scotland was so worrying. Pym and his allies were well aware that there was still frequent talk at court of the king's regaining his power by armed force. They could not make their knowledge public without revealing their sources, so had to find ways, using information already in the public domain, to persuade the Commons to endorse the measures they regarded as essential: subjecting the king's command of the armed forces and choice of counsellors to Parliamentary control. At that time the majority of the House were not sufficiently fearful of imminent danger to overcome their innate respect for the king's prerogatives. That was soon to change.

The other nagging, unresolved issue was religion. The bill to abolish bishops had caused heated debate in the Commons and was eventually abandoned. The Commons did pass a bill to exclude the bishops from the House of Lords, where they were seen as forming a bloc of votes favourable to the king; the Lords rejected the bill, not least because they resented the Commons trying to change the composition of their House. Meanwhile, anxiety grew, in the House and outside, at iconoclasm in the parish churches, ministers failing to use the Prayer Book services and the proliferation of gathered churches. As Laudianism was smashed or fell into disuse, traditional Prayer Book Anglicans felt that change had gone too far and was happening much too fast. The traditional church had particularly powerful defenders in the House of Lords. The Lords were prepared to act quickly and decisively to ensure the safety of the kingdom – after the revelation of the army plot, for example. But the lay peers – not to mention the bishops – were not prepared to promote the Commons' brand of godly reformation. Thus in September, as we have seen, when the Commons ordered the removal from churches of altar rails and 'superstitious' objects, the Lords reissued an earlier order that divine service should be celebrated in the churches according to law. In this the Lords were more in tune with public opinion than the Commons were. Changes in the parish churches were much resented (as were the taxes needed to disband the army), and there were reports of attacks on 'godly' ministers and derogatory remarks about 'sectaries'. The Junto, earlier seen as 'patriots', were now seen as a Puritan oligarchy, bent on monopolizing power and imposing their own sour brand of godliness on a reluctant nation.

In general, however, the recess was a period of relative calm. In Scotland Charles pursued a typically convoluted and devious strategy of trying to conciliate the Covenanters with (probably insincere) concessions, while trying to exploit the growing resentment of the Covenanters' authoritarianism and extremism to build up an anti-Covenanter party. He was so immersed in these intrigues, and so hopeful of success, that he allowed the English Parliament to reconvene on 20 October. It was never wise for a king to allow Parliament to meet in his absence and on this occasion two developments, one of them his doing, the other outside his control, played into his opponents' hands. The first occurred in Scotland, where negotiations between the king and the Covenanters seemed likely to founder on the demand that the Scottish Parliament should nominate the king's leading ministers in Scotland. A group of anti-Covenanters suggested that they should arrest (and very possibly kill) the leading Covenanter nobles, headed by the marquis of Hamilton and the earl of Argyll. It is not certain that the king was implicated in this conspiracy, but it is more than probable that he was, and it was widely assumed in England that it represented a continuation of the army plot. It offered further evidence that any 'concessions' made by the king were worthless. The news of the Incident (as it was called) broke in England just as Parliament was assembling. Dramatic accounts of this 'bloody conspiracy' quickly appeared in the press. Pym quickly linked it to the popish plot and the army plot in order to sustain the sense of danger, which could be used to justify curtailing or denying meaningful debate. The

Houses, fearful of a similar coup, ordered that a guard be posted around the Parliament buildings day and night.

Worse was to follow, from the king's point of view. On 31 October news arrived of a major rebellion in Ireland. Since 1603 Catholics, particular the Gaelic Irish, had gradually been deprived of their lands, which had then been granted to English and Scottish Protestants, who were encouraged to bring over settlers, to change the ethnic balance of the population. Catholics had also been increasingly excluded from public offices and from Parliament. This had particularly affected the Old English, Catholics of English descent, who still regarded themselves as English and who formed the traditional ruling class in Ireland. Charles I had offered to secure the estates of Catholic landowners in return for money, but had never delivered on his promise, and Strafford had speeded up the process of confiscation, especially in the western province of Connacht. Catholics from Ireland initially contributed to the proceedings against Strafford, but soon became alarmed at the turn of events in England. Catholics and Protestants from Ireland could unite in condemning Strafford's arbitrary and illegal behaviour, but some of the charges made against him by Protestants concerned his alleged favour to Catholics. The most ominous development, from the Catholic point of view, was the cooperation between the English and Scottish Parliaments and their well-publicized commitment to eradicate popery in all three kingdoms. The Catholic delegates from the Irish Parliament, who had come to testify against Strafford, returned home deeply anxious. They believed that the king was basically friendly, but they increasingly doubted whether he any longer had the power to protect them against his Protestant subjects.

As news of the situation in England spread through Ireland, amid fears of an Anglo-Scottish Protestant crusade against popery, the native Irish of Ulster decided that their only hope was a pre-emptive strike. They rose in arms against the Protestant landowners and clergy; many were killed, title deeds and Protestant homes were burned. Men and women were stripped and beaten and their homes were plundered. Protestant churches, Bibles and prayer books were desecrated; recently buried corpses were dug up and dumped by the roadside, or reburied face down, in the belief that their souls would then go down to hell. The violence spread south into Leinster, the province which included Dublin, where the Old English were most numerous. They had a strong tradition of service and loyalty to the English crown, but now it was a moot point whether the king was in control of his kingdom. The English authorities in Dublin launched indiscriminate reprisals against Catholics, killing many hundreds. Sharing the fears of the Gaelic Irish, and believing that they might well be killed and their estates plundered if they held aloof, many of the Old English joined the rising.[1]

News of the Irish rising caused panic in England. Many Protestants were indeed killed by the insurgents, but the figures were greatly inflated by the English press and there were innumerable stories of appalling atrocities. Apart from shock and horror at what was happening in Ireland, the rising raised in an acute form a question which the majority in Parliament had hitherto been able to shelve, that of control of the army. It was generally accepted that an army would have to be raised to put down the rising: indeed, the Scottish Parliament had already resolved to raise one. But the king's English army had been disbanded, to general relief. Memories of the army plot were still vivid and, two days before news of the Irish rising arrived, Pym had revealed details of a second army plot. Back in June the king had encouraged army officers to subscribe a petition against the unreasonable demands being made of him by persons who challenged his authority and raised tumults. Members of both Houses had to ask themselves whether Charles I, with his present advisers, could be trusted with an army. Once he had one, might he not use it against Parliament? And, if he could not be trusted, what was Parliament to do about it? The logical answer, from the point of view of Pym and his allies, was that the king should share his

control of the army with Parliament and submit his nomina-
tions for ministerial office to Parliament for approval. Charles
had conceded the latter point in Scotland, after the Incident.
He was always prepared to concede more to the Scots:
Scotland mattered less to him than England and he was
confident that, once he had restored his authority in England,
he could renege on any concessions made in Scotland. But the
English House of Commons was reluctant to accept Pym's
logic. Shortly before news of the Irish rising broke, it had
rejected a proposal that Parliament should have a veto on the
king's choice of ministers. On 5 November, after the news
broke, the Commons rejected a proposal that Parliament
should do nothing about Ireland unless the king removed
those designated by Parliament as evil counsellors.

On 8 November Pym tried again. His previous proposal had
probably upset MPs who fervently believed that something
had to be done about Ireland, and quickly. He now introduced
a changed proposal: that unless the king removed evil counsellors, Parliament should provide for Ireland without him.
This was in many ways a more radical proposal, in that the
making of peace and war was one of the king's most basic
prerogatives; but it was approved by the Commons (although
not by the Lords). This approval probably owed something to
the fact that Parliament had already begun to perform executive functions, including raising a small force for Ireland,
since the king had announced his intention to go to Scotland. It
owed more to desperate concern for the English settlers and a
deep conviction that the king could not be trusted with an
army. For Pym the Commons' resolution was a major success,
but he knew that it was most unlikely that the Lords and king
would concur with it, unless they were put under sustained
pressure from outside. To this end, he reverted to the tactics
used to secure the destruction of Strafford: mobilizing enough
popular support to scare not only the king but also the Lords
into compliance. The Junto had already tried to weaken their
opponents in the Lords, by passing the bishops' exclusion bill

and impeaching thirteen bishops. But the Lords had not passed the exclusion bill and ignored demands to suspend the impeached bishops, or exclude the Catholic peers. In pursuit of this same end, also on 8 November, the Commons gave a first reading to the Grand Remonstrance, a lengthy indictment of the conduct of government since 1625, followed by a programme of reform.

The Grand Remonstrance had first been planned in the later stages of Strafford's trial. A substantial draft had been completed by August; now the Irish rising and the second army plot provided additional 'evidence' of the conspiracy. In many ways, it reiterated the analysis of the ills of the kingdom which Pym had given the Commons almost exactly a year before: the most striking change was that the Irish rising could now be cited as proof of the existence of the popish plot, and there can be little doubt that Pym believed this. Now, however, the analysis was developed at much greater length. The authors of the plot were identified as 'the Jesuited papists', 'the bishops and the corrupt part of the clergy', and malevolent counsellors and courtiers.[2] The remedies that the Remonstrance proposed for the ills of the kingdom included the summoning of a general synod of the most learned divines 'of this island', 'assisted with some from foreign parts, professing the same religion with us', to consider the further reform of the English Church: the intention clearly was to bring England into line with the Scottish and continental Calvinist churches.[3] It concluded with a call on the king to appoint such counsellors 'as the Parliament may have cause to confide in'; if he did not do so, the Commons would feel unable to supply him with money. It stressed that the Commons could object to men nominated by the king even if there was no proof of wrong-doing on their part.[4]

This was most emphatically a manifesto, not a petition to the king. It was, in fact, presented to the king on 1 December, accompanied by a petition. This denied any intention of criticizing the king: its purpose was to 'represent how your royal authority and trust have been abused, to the great prejudice and danger of your majesty and of all your good subjects'.[5] This disclaimer must have sounded hollow in the light of the Commons' resolution nine days earlier to approve the Remonstrance. The resolution passed by only eleven votes in a full House, after an angry debate in which swords were drawn and MPs stressed the dangers of referring to the king as a third person, 'remonstrating downwards' and telling tales to the people. For the main purpose of the Remonstrance was undoubtedly to rally popular support against the king. On the night of the vote a thousand men remained in Westminster Yard. Some claimed that they had been summoned by some MPs and that their masters had given them swords; they were fearful that the 'best affected party' might lose the vote.[6] The Commons' adoption of the Grand Remonstrance drastically raised the stakes in what was becoming an increasingly open struggle for power between the king and his opponents. At the same time, the Commons were becoming deeply divided, and there was a similar division between the majorities in the Commons and in the Lords. When the Commons voted to print the Remonstrance some of the defeated minority claimed that members of the Lower House had a right (like the peers) to enter protests against resolutions of which they particularly disapproved.

The size of the vote against the Remonstrance showed that the king now enjoyed a level of political support that he had patently lacked a year earlier. This was not due to any action on his part. It has been remarked that he gained most support when he did least, and at times he seemed almost perversely determined to drive away potential supporters by rash and ill-considered actions. At the time of the vote on the Grand Remonstrance he had not yet returned from Scotland, and when he returned to London on 25 November he was accompanied and welcomed by a large number of 'cavaliers', or 'reformadoes', swaggering army officers, who had come to London after the disbanding of the Northern army to demand their pay. They volunteered to defend his person and made their contempt for the citizens abundantly clear. When the king made his formal entry in to the City, at the invitation of the new lord mayor, the tone was heavily military. His escort included many of the City militia and the Honourable Artillery Company, but also many reformadoes. He did take some steps to reassure the public, stressing his opposition to innovation in the Church and the urgency of suppressing the Irish rising, and seeking to win over the rulers of the City of London. But at the same time signs continued that he intended to appeal to force. Pym continued to produce revelations about the second army plot, but Charles's own actions also suggested that he planned some sort of coup. Essex's commission to command the forces south of the Trent expired with the king's return and was not renewed. The king also ordered the removal of the guard appointed by Essex for the two Houses during the king's absence. If, despite this, he gained more support in Parliament and outside, this reflected growing anxiety about the direction and implications of Pym's political programme and methods.

Many MPs resented Pym's tactics within Parliament. His anti-popish rhetoric led to his supporters being depicted as the only good Protestants and his critics as papists or favourers of popery. Those whom he castigated as 'delinquents' (notably the bishops) were harassed. These were divisive tactics and Pym was ruthless in forcing divisions, or votes. Votes are an integral part of modern British parliamentary practice, but in early seventeenth-century Parliaments they were comparatively rare, and were regarded with distaste. The preference was for members to talk their way to a widely acceptable (or at least not too widely unacceptable) consensus (as in elections). There was a deep suspicion of the majority trying to coerce the minority. There were issues of principle, too. Edward Hyde had been a vigorous critic of the measures and ministers of the Personal Rule, but by the end of 1641 he was convinced that Pym's aim was to strip the king of his powers and reduce him to a cipher. Hyde became one of the king's most influential advisers. He was not alone in fearing that the ancient constitution was being overturned. Others were worried by threats of religious change. The Remonstrance itself offered the prospect, unpalatable for many, of Scottish-style Presbyterianism, but of more concern still was the emergence of separatist sects and the prospect of religious anarchy. Most worrying of all, and prominent in the debates on printing the Remonstrance, was the fear that appealing to the people could lead to anarchy and the destruction of all law and property. This fear was stoked by the Protestation and the Commons' growing practice of passing and printing highly partisan 'votes'. For Hyde and many more, an effective king was needed to shore up the existing social and political order and to maintain the traditional constitution and the rule of law. They saw attacks on 'cavaliers' as attacks on the landed elite generally. Petitions to Parliament had become increasingly threatening; some were accompanied by large crowds, others warned that the petitioners were desperate, with clear hints of violence if grievances were not redressed: 'hunger will break through stone walls'. Faced with such dangers, the king could be cast in the role of an essentially conservative, but also benevolent and law-abiding figure. To some extent he was prepared to play this role, and showed himself aware of the revulsion against the Junto's methods. On 12 December he issued a proclamation summoning absent members of both Houses to appear at Westminster by 12 January. This raised the real possibility that the Junto's majority in the Commons would be overturned, and the majority against it in the Lords would be reinforced. If that were to happen, the king would be perfectly placed to wreak revenge on his opponents, without the need to appeal to force.

While the Grand Remonstrance was passing through the Commons, Pym and his allies took steps to wrest control of the militia from the king. On 16 November, following further revelations about the second army plot, the Commons ordered that the militia should be prepared for action. It also ordered the arrest of a number of leading Catholics, which it had no legal authority to do. The Lords refused to concur, but agreed to expel the Catholic peers. Events again came to Pym's aid at the beginning of December, when news came that one of the Irish rebels, Sir Phelim O'Neill, claimed to have a commission from the king to take up arms. The 'commission' was in fact a forgery: the seal attached to it had been taken from another document. But it convinced many Irish Catholics that the king approved the rising and would have supported it openly if he could. (O'Neill was executed in 1652, after the Cromwellian conquest of Ireland, because he refused to declare that the commission had been genuine.) In England the news of the 'commission' further damaged the king's political credibility, and on 7 December a bill was brought into the Commons to transfer power over the militia and the armed forces from the king to persons acceptable to Parliament. There was another bill to allow the impressment of soldiers (but not the raising of volunteers) for Ireland, which would mean that the king could not raise forces without Parliament's consent; it would also prevent him from gathering a force of reformadoes. The tension, in London and elsewhere, was almost unbearable. There were wild rumours that the Irish had landed in the North, or that the papists were about to rise up and cut the Protestants' throats. Londoners felt especially threatened and their attention focused on the Lords, whose reluctance to join the Commons in measures for the public safety was blamed on the bishops and the Catholic peers. A petition for their removal was said to have 15,000 signatures. In an attempt to incite popular feeling still further, a motion to print the Grand Remonstrance (which also blamed the bishops and the Catholic peers) was rushed through the Commons late in the evening in a thin House. On 21 December the Commons publicly blamed the Lords for obstructing the relief of Ireland.

The day-to-day government of the City was carried on by the lord mayor and aldermen, who served for life. Many citizens believed that the aldermen were not taking sufficient steps to protect them from these dangers, and resented the warm welcome which the lord mayor and aldermen had organized for the king on his return from Scotland. Londoners showed their anger and frustration in the annual elections for the City's common council on 21 December. The common council played no part in the City's government; its role was confined to approving rates and accounts and passing by-laws. Because its role was limited, elections were usually uncontentious and uneventful; but this was not so in 1641. The contest was vigorous and the end product was a common council in which a majority strongly favoured the analysis of events, and the measures, of Pym and his allies.

For the king, the common council election results were deeply worrying. They showed that disaffection (as he saw it) was rife in the capital and he feared insurrection. It made control of the Tower vital and he was not inclined to trust either the constable (Newport) or his lieutenant (Sir William Balfour). He dismissed Balfour and appointed in his place a particularly thuggish army officer, Colonel Thomas Lunsford. Panic spread through the City. The Tower was much the biggest arsenal in the country and there were fears that Lunsford could use the artillery there to shell the City and reduce it to rubble. Citizens watched all night, with weapons in their hands, and took to the streets in their thousands. The London homes of bishops were attacked. Soon even Charles realized that Lunsford's appointment was a mistake; although he was removed on the 26th, at the lord mayor's request, the damage had been done. Armed 'cavaliers' still milled around the court, determined to defend the king's person; some five hundred of them were accommodated in a makeshift barracks in Whitehall. They clashed with apprentices, who were also armed. Cavaliers also swarmed around outside Parliament. As the cavaliers became more numerous and aggressive, towards the end of December, the clashes became more violent: it was said that several Londoners were killed on 29 December, after which the king pointedly feasted the cavaliers, who by now were using the term 'roundhead' to describe their opponents. The king posted a larger guard at Whitehall Palace, under the command of Lunsford: he too feared for his safety. The new lieutenant of the Tower, Sir John Byron, increased the size of the garrison.

The tensions in the streets were replicated within Parliament. On the 24th the Commons read the militia bill for the second time and asked the Lords to join them in warning of the dangers from papists and other 'malignants' – presumably including Lunsford. There were wild rumours of a popish insurrection, similar to that in Ireland, and foreign invasion. When the Lords refused, the Commons resolved that any blood spilt as a result of their refusal would be on the Lords' hands. The Houses argued about who was to guard them, and against whom: ruffianly cavaliers or crowds of fearful, angry citizens. Attention focused on the bishops. The Catholics had ceased to attend, but many of those bishops who were not in prison continued to do so, and were very visible in their epis-copal vestments. On 27 December they ran the gauntlet of an angry crowd; the next day only two managed to enter. The Londoners had done what all the resolutions of the Commons had failed to do – broken the anti-Junto majority in the Lords. The Commons pointedly failed to condemn the crowd's actions. On the 29th twelve of the bishops presented a protest to the Lords in which they claimed that any action taken in the House in their absence, or under duress from the crowds, was null and void. The Lords were furious that one group of peers should seek to dictate to the rest of the House, and passed the protest to the Commons, who impeached the twelve on charges of treason; the Lords ordered that they should be imprisoned. Some in the Commons proposed that the House should adjourn to Guildhall, to ensure its safety, and Pym moved that it should ask for a guard of the City militia. The next day chanting crowds at Whitehall were driven off, with swords, by cavaliers.

Despite the Lords' angry reaction to the bishops' protest, substantial minorities in both Houses were becoming extremely anxious about the direction of events, especially the

Commons' challenges to the king's prerogatives and the efforts of London crowds to dictate to Parliament; they were doubly worried by the Commons' eagerness to incite the crowds to action by means of partisan resolutions. In this situation the king's wisest course would have been to do nothing provocative and allow this conservative backlash to gather momentum, with the prospect that the situation might change dramatically once the absent members returned. But there was also a real possibility that by the time that happened the Houses would have taken drastic steps to reduce the king to a cipher, and this was not a risk that he was prepared to take. He was convinced that most MPs were loyal and well-meaning, but were swayed by a few demagogic trouble-makers who aimed to deprive him of his lawful authority; so he decided to take them out. He drew up an 'impeachment' in which he accused Pym and four others of treasonously plotting to deprive him of his regal power and to alienate the affections of his subjects. They had encouraged a foreign army (the Scots) to invade England, had raised tumults and had levied war against the king. The charges included the now obligatory reference to the 'fundamental laws'.[7]

For the king to take his stand on the traditional constitution made sound political sense, as did the charge that the five had incited popular disorder. If he was going to proceed against them, it was appropriate, indeed essential, that he should do so using the law. He may have expected the Lords to take their judicial role in this impeachment as seriously as they had in Strafford's; he may simply have been trying to divert the Houses' attention from his own powers. Whatever his expectations, they were disappointed. When his charges against the five were read to the Lords, their only response was to appoint a committee to consider whether he could legally bring an impeachment. Their lack of response drove the king to take more violent, and less legal, measures. That night the king decided to follow up his charge by arresting the five in the House of Commons itself. He may have been encouraged in this by the queen, who was always exhorting him to exert his authority, or he may have felt that a show of force was necessary; there were rumours that the queen was to be impeached. Either way, his plan went disastrously wrong. It had been the talk of the court, and news soon reached the MPs themselves, perhaps from Lady Carlisle, perhaps from the French ambassador. When, on 4 January 1642, Charles burst into the House of Commons with four hundred unruly armed men, the five were nowhere to be seen. When Charles asked the speaker where they were, the speaker replied that as the servant of the House he could say nothing without its direction. The king's bravado quickly turned to embarrassment and he slunk out of the House with cries of 'privilege of Parliament', from both MPs and the crowds outside, ringing in his ears.

It would have been difficult for Charles to find a more effective way of uniting the House of Commons. Even the most conservative members were outraged at this invasion of their privileges; some believed that the cavaliers would have slaughtered them if they had offered any resistance. But Charles's folly did not end there: he also impeached one of the Lords, Lord Mandeville. The peers were equally incensed; and so at a time when there was still a prospect of playing on the Lords' resentment of Pym's policies and tactics, and of setting the Lords against the Commons, Charles united the two Houses against him. Together they had already asked the City to send a detachment of its trained bands (militia) to guard them, a clear indication that they did not trust the king's guards.

For the king, this was not the worst. The attempt to arrest the five members was widely seen as the first step of a long anticipated military coup. Panic spread through London. The citizens regarded the lord mayor and aldermen as too friendly, or subservient, to the king, and did not trust him to protect their lives, liberty and property. On the morning of 4 January, before the king came to the Commons, the House had appealed to the City authorities for aid. The common council assembled, without a summons from the lord mayor, and set up a committee of safety, which took over control of the government of the City. At some stage before 5 January, either the common council or the committee of safety had replaced the existing commanders of the City militia with men who supported the Commons leadership.[8] The City's government and armed forces were now totally outside the king's (and indeed the lord mayor's) control; the lord mayor was assaulted after conducting the king out of the City, and his mayoral chain was ripped from his neck. The Commons, claiming that they were not safe at Westminster, reconvened at Guildhall, with a large guard of trained bands, who also patrolled the streets. When the king came to the City, and appeared before the common council, on the 5th, he met with an openly hostile reception. He became even more fearful for the safety of his family, and especially of the queen. As unrest continued, he decided to leave London. He slipped away to Hampton Court on 10 January. He was not to return until he was brought to London for his trial.

When news came that the king had gone, the Commons returned to Westminster in triumph, escorted by the trained bands, many of whom had the Protestation on their hats. The king had suffered his most significant defeat of the civil war, losing his capital, more than six months before hostilities formally started. London contained a tenth of England's population and handled some two-thirds of its overseas trade; it also contained much the largest concentration of moneyed wealth and the nation's only money market. On top of all that, it was the centre of government. In leaving London, Charles left Parliament in control of the regular institutions of government, while he travelled the provinces trying to attract supporters, like a medieval rebel baron.

Charles probably had little clear idea of what to do next: he was just convinced that he would not be safe in London. He hoped eventually to reassert his authority by force, but at present he was far too weak to do so, having nothing resembling an army. He decided to appoint reliable men to command key fortresses, particularly that at Hull, whose magazine contained many of the weapons from the army raised against the Scots, and to secure Portsmouth, but Parliament was too quick for him and secured both. The Commons took the lead in this; the Lords agreed that magazines should be secured, and the militia mobilized, under the command of men on whom Parliament could rely, but they would not at first demand that the king should place forts in the hands of men whom Parliament could trust. The Lords were always more willing to take steps to meet the immediate threat of violence from the king than to endorse lasting constitutional or religious change: those who had sat on the privy council in the past knew from personal experience how devious and unscrupulous the king could be. The Lords were the more willing to act because the measures they endorsed could be seen as defensive: if Parliament could defend itself, surely the king would have to come to terms with it. For Pym, however, short-term security was not the solution: the king needed to be stripped of the power to harm his people. He did what he could to thwart moves by the Commons to reach an accommodation with the king, who (fortunately for Pym) had no interest in compromise. At the same time, Pym used mass petitions and demonstrations to intimidate the Lords: he stressed that the peers could not expect any protection from the City militia, now firmly under the control of the committee of safety.

The public mood remained volatile and angry. Trade and manufactures were depressed, food prices were high, unemployment was widespread. On 1 February a large crowd of women assembled at Westminster, declaring that they had no food for their children and blaming the Lords for their refusal to suppress popery and idolatry.[9] Popular pressure, encouraged and to some extent orchestrated by the Commons leaders, gradually told, helped by the gradual departure of Royalist peers to join the king. The Lords finally agreed to pass the bishops' exclusion bill (which further shifted the political balance in the House) and also the militia bill, which gave

Parliament the power to appoint the lords lieutenant and deputy lieutenants of the county militias, which were still seen as the nation's primary defence force. The king refused to give his assent to this bill, although he did agree to the bishops' exclusion bill, under the influence of the queen, for whom all types of Protestant church were equally false. He also gave his assent to the adventurers' bill, which ordered the confiscation of over two million acres of land belonging to Irish 'rebels', which could be sold to recoup the cost of (eventually) reconquering Ireland. His refusal to pass the militia bill meant that the militia ordinance (as it was called) was issued on the authority of the two Houses only. This was of course a break with constitutional tradition – the king's assent had always been required for making laws – but necessity dictated that the Houses had to take control of the militia in order to defend themselves. They did not, as yet, claim the power to impose taxes without the king's concurrence.

As the months went on, the king realized that the government had not collapsed without him. More and more peers and MPs joined him from Westminster, but he still had far too little support to embark on a war. Many of those who joined him urged him to come to terms with Parliament. When he moved to York, thinking he would find more support in the North, many of the Yorkshire gentry, and a large assembly of freeholders, gave him similar advice, which he had no intention of taking. Encouraged by the queen, he schemed to secure military help from abroad. He sent emissaries to Denmark and the queen pawned the crown jewels and endeavoured to persuade Frederick Henry, prince of Orange, to send part of the Dutch army to aid the king. But the Dutch were still preoccupied with their war of independence against Spain and even the offer to marry the prince of Wales to Frederick Henry's daughter was not enough to secure meaningful Dutch help. (The prince's sister, Mary, had married Frederick Henry's son, William, the previous year.) Charles also sought military help from Scotland – he remained pathetically convinced that, outside London, his subjects loved him – and talked of going to Ireland to suppress the rebellion; his opponents, naturally, suspected that his true aim was to put himself at the head of the Irish Catholic rebels. In all these schemes, Hull played a crucial part, as a convenient port at which to land Danish or Dutch troops and a source of arms, vital for the king's proposed expedition to Ireland. The queen repeatedly badgered him to take possession of Hull. He had appointed the earl of Newcastle governor of the town, but Parliament had given the post to Sir John Hotham, who had taken command of the town, with orders to secure it against all comers. On 23 April, the king finally came to the town, believing that Hotham would admit him if he appeared in person, but the gates remained firmly closed against him. Thwarted and humiliated, he had no alternative but to proclaim Hotham a traitor and withdraw.

Meanwhile, king and Parliament were fighting a propaganda war through the press and the pulpit. This was partly a battle for hearts and minds, partly an attempt to apportion blame for what had gone wrong over the previous two years. Parliament took the more systematic approach to propaganda, and tried to send copies of its votes and declarations to every parish in the country. The king promised that in future he would govern according to law and protect the Protestant religion, as by law established, against papists and sectaries. Parliament argued that the king was in the thrall of 'malignant' counsellors who would not allow him to deliver on such promises. But not all were convinced of the threat from the papists and denounced the 'faction of malignant, schismatical and ambitious persons, whose design is ... to alter the whole frame of government, both of Church and State, and to subject both king and people to their own lawless arbitrary power'.[10] To add to their sense of unease, rural disorders continued, as people violently sought to reverse enclosures and to wreck fen drainage schemes, or raided deer parks; some claimed that there was now no law.

Parliament ordered that all adult males should subscribe to the Protestation: it wished to know who its friends, and its enemies, were. A bill to that effect had passed the Commons in July 1641, but had been rejected by the Lords. The Commons now resolved that those refusing to subscribe were unfit for office. The Commons showed an increasing concern to weed out and expel 'neuters' from the House, while blood-curdling sermons from godly preachers tried to stir the House to a pitch of militant zeal. The issues were debated in the alehouse and the market place, sometimes with angry words and blows: 'foul language and desperate quarrellings even between old and entire friends'.[11] The torrent of petitions continued unabated, but now their content reflected the growing divisions in the nation. There were still petitions for godly reformation and against popery, but also petitions defending episcopacy and the Prayer Book liturgy. The Church of England clergy were especially active in promoting such petitions and in opposing the Protestation. A petition from Kent, a county which had earlier produced a major petition for root and branch, declared: 'The houses of God are profaned and in part defaced; the ministers of Christ are condemned and despised; the ornaments and many utensils of the church are abused; the liturgy and book of common prayer depraved and neglected.'[12] This petition, and many others, stressed that the Church's worship and government were allowed by custom and tradition, but were now being overthrown by the fancies of individuals.

Fear of bloody strife was now very real indeed. As soon as the king left London the Commons issued a declaration advising people to prepare to defend themselves. Towns repaired their fortifications and bought weapons; so did many private individuals. As early as January 1642 the Shrewsbury Drapers' Company resolved to cancel its annual Easter feast and to spend the money saved on buying arms and relieving the poor.[13] On 20 May the Houses declared that the king intended to make war on them and demanded that he desist from raising troops; if he did not, they would do their utmost to maintain the public peace.[14] As Parliament grew in self-confidence (or desperation), its demands to the king became more extreme, culminating in the Nineteen Propositions of 2 June. These included the demand that the nomination of all privy councillors, judges and officers should be approved by Parliament, that all matters of state should be considered by the privy council, and that all who advised a particular course of action should put their names to it; here at last was an effective, if radical, way of resolving the problem of identifying 'evil counsellors'. Parliament was to supervise the education, and approve the marriages, of the king's children. The Church was to be reformed as advised by the two Houses. Those identified by Parliament as 'delinquents' should be handed over to Parliament for punishment. The king was to enter into alliances with the Dutch and other Protestant powers to defend the Protestant religion against popery. Catholic peers were to be excluded from the Lords and no new peers were to be admitted without the consent of both Houses. If the king agreed to all these demands (and more), Parliament would settle on him a revenue 'sufficient to support your royal dignity in honour and plenty'.[15]

There was no prospect whatever that the king would agree to these demands, which would reduce him to the merest cipher and deprive him of the rights enjoyed by his subjects: what father would renounce his authority over the education and marriage of his children? The king's published answer to the Nineteen Propositions did not condescend to respond to them in detail, but instead addressed what he saw as the dangers implicit in Parliament's conduct. At the heart of his answer was a clear commitment to a mixed and balanced constitution, which combined the merits, but avoided the drawbacks, of monarchy, aristocracy and democracy. This mixture and balance were being threatened, he said, by the Commons' appeal to the people in order to exalt itself at the expense of the Lords and king. Such a strategy was cynical, but also dangerous. Having built up the power of the people, and shown them their strength, it would be difficult to prevent them from seizing power and overthrowing all three elements in the constitution.

Sooner or later, he concluded, the common people would realize 'that all this is done by them, but not for them' and 'set up for themselves'. They would then 'destroy all rights and proprieties [properties], all distinctions of families and merit, and by this means this splendid and excellently distinguished form of government end in a dark equal chaos of confusion'.[16]

The answer to the Nineteen Propositions was the most explicit and forceful attempt to date to present Charles as a responsible and above all constitutional monarch. Divine-right monarchy, and its implications, were quietly forgotten, but such an approach did not meet with universal approval among the king's advisers. The queen, for a start, argued that the monarchy would be secure only if it was absolute, and her views were shared by some of the king's English supporters. Moreover, the king's record did not suggest that he would be comfortable in the role of a responsible constitutional monarch, which was one reason why many who came to join him urged him to come to terms with Parliament. To regain his power he needed an army, and not nearly enough volunteers had come to join him. There was no eagerness for war in the provinces in the first half of 1642 – just the reverse. People watched with bewilderment and alarm as events unfolded in London and the king left his capital. Many even in Parliament were torn both ways: they respected the king's authority and valued the ancient constitution; they loathed Laudianism, but feared sectarianism and religious anarchy, 'breaking asunder the well-ordered chain of government';[17] they abhorred the king's willingness to resort to force, but feared the consequences of empowering the crowds. As one Norfolk MP remarked, 'whensoever necessity shall enforce us to make use of the multitude, I do not promise myself safety'.[18] Both sides claimed to stand for the just rights of both king and Parliament. In July 1642 Sir Benjamin Rudyerd made a speech in the Commons in which he enumerated the achievements of Parliament in dismantling the Personal Rule, expressing regret that many were still not satisfied, and pinpointing the reason:

'we stand chiefly upon future security'. 'Let us save our liberties and our estates, as [provided] we may save our souls too.'[19] Or, as the earl of Northumberland put it: 'the alteration of government is apprehended on both sides'; 'neither king nor Parliament are without fears and jealousies, the one of having his authority and just rights invaded, the other of losing that liberty which freeborn subjects ought to enjoy and the laws of the land do allow us'.[20] Sir Edward Dering, once a vocal supporter of root and branch, now wrote that he 'did not like one side or the other so well as to join myself with either. A composing third way was my wish and my prayer.'[21] Faced with a stark choice between the threat of tyranny and the spectre of anarchy, it is not surprising that many tried to find a middle way, or to keep out. If this was true of Rudyerd at Westminster, it was even more true of many in the provinces, for whom the issues were less clear: many petitions to Parliament called on it to reach agreement with the king. Meetings for county business were marked by anxious discussions of how to keep the war away.

It came a step nearer in June. The king's supporters had tried to take control of the militia, with limited success, so the king issued commissions of array to gentlemen whom he hoped were loyal to him, and ordered the militia to obey these commanders rather than those appointed by Parliament. Both king and Parliament were trying to gain control of the militia, and its weapons. The commissions of array were a medieval device for raising soldiers; they were legal, but unfamiliar, and the fact that they were in Latin enabled Parliament to misrepresent their content. They seemed more novel, and threatening, than the familiar commanders of the county militia, the lords lieutenant. The king's supporters tried to offset this disadvantage by seeking endorsement from grand juries, often seen as the representative bodies of the counties. The king declared that he did not intend to make war, but simply to defend himself; the fact that he was trying to secure military support from Scotland and Holland would suggest that he was not entirely sincere. Unfortunately, he initially had more men than weapons and so seized the arms in county magazines, depriving the counties of the ability to defend themselves. His more unruly followers also alienated people by their arrogance and violence: punitive or preventive measures against those seen as hostile to the king's cause could easily degenerate into plunder (although Parliamentarian forces plundered Royalists as well).

There followed numerous local struggles for control of the local militia and magazines, and of key towns and river crossings. In some counties, notably in the East Midlands and central southern England, musters were summoned under the militia ordinance; in others (for example in the West Midlands) they were summoned under commissions of array. Some counties, such as Lancashire and Cheshire, were bitterly contested. Much depended on the energy, commitment and popularity of individual peers, gentlemen and MPs. Apart from enlisting their own tenants, they also encouraged volunteers. Townsmen were initially more inclined to see Royalists as outsiders, and a threat; Parliament's agents tended to encourage towns to arm to defend themselves. In Shrewsbury attempts by Parliament's supporters to mobilize the militia were frustrated by the mayor and a Royalist mob, but when both sides began to drill, the corporation forbade the wearing of partisan badges. Later the town was secured by Sir Richard Newport and other Royalist notables.[22]

On 17 June the earl of Newcastle, with a force consisting of county militias and his own tenants, seized Newcastle for the king, at last giving him a substantial port where troops from the Continent could be landed. Courtiers were confident that the king's fortunes were now in the ascendant and expressed hopes of getting rich on forfeited 'rebel' estates.[23] Gifts from Royalist peers, led by the immensely rich earl of Worcester, provided the money the king would need to pay an army. Worcester was a Catholic and many of the king's most active supporters were Catholics, who had more to fear than any other group from a Parliamentarian victory. Charles also tried, unsuccessfully, to secure the fleet, which instead declared for Parliament. Local Royalist successes worried Parliament; on 6 July it voted to raise an army of 10,000 men, over and above the militia, under the command of the earl of Essex. It was recruited mainly in the south-east, and especially in London. The Commons also appointed a committee of safety, entrusted with doing whatever was necessary for the defence of Parliament and the safety of the kingdom. This followed the precedent set in London in January and was to be the first of numerous committees that performed the various executive functions necessary for the war effort. It received news from the provinces, and passed on to the Commons only as much as it judged fit. Parliament (or rather the committee of safety) now unashamedly took control of the government. It looked to individual MPs to promote the war effort in their localities: increasingly members became the agents of the centre.

Conflict in the provinces gradually proliferated. The first fatality occurred at Manchester on 15 July and the first significant engagement at Marshall's Elm in Somerset on 4 August. Portsmouth was secured for the king early in August, but taken by Parliament on 7 September. Attempts to win support for the Royalists in Leicestershire proved largely unsuccessful and the king failed to secure Coventry, although he appeared there in person; he was also rebuffed again at Hull. A state of war now effectively existed and Parliament, on 2 August, issued a declaration of its reasons for taking up arms, in which it denied it was behaving in any way arbitrarily or illegally. On 9 August all members of the Commons were required to swear that they would support the earl of Essex to the death. However, even though there were substantial bodies of armed men in the provinces, their commanders often tried to avoid coming to blows. The king's advisers decided that his standard had to be set up, to rally his supporters. After some debate it was decided to set it up at Nottingham on the 22nd. The standard was carried out from the castle and set in the ground to the sound of trumpets. A proclamation was read declaring Essex a traitor;

the crowd responded with cheers and derogatory remarks about 'roundheads'. (Unfortunately the standard blew down that night.)[24] The English civil war had formally begun.

5

THE FIRST CIVIL WAR

The war that was formally begun at Nottingham was a complex affair. Alongside the field armies and the few decisive battles, there were a multiplicity of local conflicts, skirmishes and sieges. Few counties, mostly in the south-east, saw no fighting at all, and some, like Somerset or Wiltshire, were fought over continually. As was often the case in the seventeenth century, much time was spent in peace negotiations while the war continued. At first only a small minority of people actively supported one side or the other. Many hoped to prevent the war from touching their locality by means of neutrality pacts. In Staffordshire and Lincolnshire a third force was created, to keep the war away and to maintain order. But in time the divisions became deeper and more pervasive. Leading figures in town and countryside were pressed to declare for one side or the other, or to provide money, provisions or horses. Humbler folk, too, became aware of the issues, as they were rehearsed in the pulpit, the press and the alehouse. Many, however, were to change sides as local circumstances, or their perception of the issues, changed. Each side projected negative images of the other. The Royalists were depicted as showily dressed drunken libertines, given to wenching and profane swearing; if they had any religion at all, they were probably papists. The Parliamentarians were portrayed as outwardly godly hypocrites, killjoys who hated the idea of anybody having a good time. They talked much of God, but saw the war as an opportunity to grow rich at the expense of others. To maintain their godly image, they dressed soberly and had their hair cut short (hence 'roundheads'). But behind the stereotypes lay the reality of very widespread commitment to one side or the other, which was why the divisions of civil war went so deep. This really was an 'unnatural' war, in that it set neighbour against neighbour, brother against brother, son against father. Not everyone wanted to take sides, of course. Some wished to keep out of the war for as long as they could. A few, like Sir John Holland, who most unusually for an MP had a Catholic wife, went abroad, but most did not have that option. Others kept their heads down, or supported the side that was stronger locally. Towns often tried to avoid committing themselves: war disrupted trade and a major siege or (still worse) sack could do enormous damage.

In assessing allegiance in the wars, it is easiest to find out about the peers and gentry, conspicuous men who were called on to declare themselves, but were also more likely to have kept correspondence and to appear in written records. These were the natural leaders of county society, but it would be a mistake to assume that their social inferiors meekly followed their lead. In Somerset the local Royalist gentry, led by the marquis of Hertford, defeated the local Parliamentarians, but were then driven out by the people. Coventry, having shut its gates when the king appeared, welcomed in Parliament's forces. The earl of Northumberland's tenants rejected point blank his summons to serve under him, and the Hastings family failed to secure Leicestershire for the king: it probably did not help that the head of the family, the earl of Huntingdon, had severe financial problems and had demanded greatly increased rents from his tenants. Some were hostile to any move that might bring the war to their locality. The earl of Worcester was more successful in mobilizing the gentry of South Wales, but the Welsh had a particular loyalty to the House of Stuart and many of the gentry (like Worcester) were Catholics. Lord Brooke in Warwickshire and the earl of Warwick in Essex were strong Puritans who recruited mainly from among the godly. Brooke installed a strong garrison in Warwick Castle and established what was in essence a private army, which he paid himself. Parliament was particularly keen to appoint peers as colonels, partly because they had the social authority and the money needed to enlist soldiers, but also to counter any claim that Parliament was overturning the natural social order; commissioning peers also helped keep the House of Lords onside.

The armies were much more than the personal retinues of great men, even on the Royalist side, where social attitudes were perhaps more traditional. There were many volunteers; some driven by principled commitment, others by the prospect of pay, plunder and adventure. The Royalists could appeal to popular loyalty to the king and the monarchy. The king was in some ways a sacred, even a magical figure, able to cure the unpleasant skin disease, scrofula, by his royal touch. All their lives people had been told that the king was God's anointed and that active resistance to his commands, or even refusal to obey him, was sinful. In fighting against the king the Parliamentarians were committing not only the heinous crime of treason, but the sin of sacrilege. The Parliamentarians countered with the argument that the king was so under the spell of his evil counsellors that he was, in effect, deranged; far from resisting him, Parliament was trying to rescue him from the clutches of those around him. Having been lawfully summoned by the king, Parliamentarians could argue that they were taking up arms by his authority against his person. Against the argument based on the divine origins of monarchy,

Parliament claimed that kings existed for the good of their people; if they threatened their people's lives, liberties and property, the people were no longer bound to obey them. The safety of the people was the supreme law; besides, the king had promised in his coronation oath to respect the laws. If he failed to do so, the people were absolved from their oaths of allegiance. The Parliamentarians, therefore, claimed to be fighting against the non-parliamentary taxation and the punishments without due process of law that had marked the 1630s.

There was also the question of religion. As the stereotype shows, the Parliamentarians were particularly identified with Puritanism. Faith gave Cromwell's troops their self-belief and sense of purpose. Believing that God constantly intervened in earthly events – that without His providence not a sparrow fell to the ground – godly Roundheads saw military victory as a mark of divine favour; they were driven by a sense that they were acting out God's will on earth. Not all Parliamentarian soldiers were godly volunteers, with a real commitment to the cause: indeed, many were conscripted. But the godly were prominent enough to shape the character of some parts of the army and the public's perception of it, particularly after the end of the first civil war. On the Royalist side religion inspired less of a sense of cause. There were few lay Laudians. A significant number of Catholics fought for the king, although fewer than his opponents made out. Their religion was less significant in forming their commitment than it was for the Puritans; rather the fact that they were Catholics, and that Parliament was so anti-Catholic, meant that there was no prospect of their fighting for Parliament. Indeed, with Parliament apparently set on destroying popery in all three kingdoms, it might well seem to English Catholics that fighting for the king was a matter of self-preservation. The factor that gave most impetus to the Royalist sense of cause was loyalty to king and to monarchy, which was especially strong in the Celtic periphery: Wales and Cornwall. Both had a particular connection with the monarchy, through the prince of Wales, who was also duke of

Cornwall. Ethnic hatred had a part to play here: Parliament's propaganda was stridently anti-Welsh (and to a lesser extent anti-Cornish).[1] Another factor in popular Royalism was hatred of Puritanism and especially Puritan hostility to popular sociability and recreation: the stereotypical Roundhead was a killjoy. The Puritan preacher Richard Baxter was twice nearly lynched in Herefordshire in late 1642 and remarked that anybody who had short hair and was soberly dressed was liable to be attacked as a 'roundhead'.[2]

The initial geographical division between the sides saw Parliament in control of the south-east and East Anglia and the Royalists strong in the North, the West Midlands, Wales and the South-west. This division reflected the simple fact that Parliament was based in London and its first priority was to establish control over the surrounding area. Although Parliament controlled a smaller area, it was richer (thanks especially to London) and there were no Royalist enclaves. Because Parliament controlled the navy, the trade of the ports of the south-east was largely uninterrupted. By contrast, there were a number of Parliamentarian towns in Royalist areas; many were reluctant to march away leaving their homes at the mercy of the enemy. The Royalists never controlled all the towns along the Severn, making it difficult to move goods or war materials through the West Midlands and Welsh Marches. The areas controlled by the Royalists were generally poorer and more sparsely populated than the south-east, and their economies suffered more disruption. Lines of communication were stretched. On the positive side, the Royalists had more experienced soldiers. Few Englishmen had any experience of war, unless they had served abroad, which a significant number of Royalists had, including Charles's cousin Rupert, a dashing cavalry commander and something of a veteran at twenty-three. Such was his reputed military prowess that it was alleged that he derived magical powers from his dog, Boy, who was shot by a Parliamentarian soldier in 1644. Most of the Parliamentarians had to learn soldiering from scratch, including Oliver Cromwell, who was then already well into his forties. The king himself had no military experience. He was personally brave, but proved an ineffective war leader. His conduct since at least 1637 had shown that he found it difficult to commit himself to a single strategy and stick to it, and he also found it hard to communicate with others. His talk of bearing affliction patiently and even of facing martyrdom can have done little to hearten his followers.

The king's war aims were simple: to defeat the Parliamentarians and regain his capital and his control of the government. Some of his followers hoped that this could be achieved without outright victory, by negotiation, on terms which preserved the reforms of 1641. Others believed that military victory was essential, if the king was to restore his authority as it had been before 1640; some indeed wanted to make the monarchy more absolute than it had ever been – and to profit from forfeited Parliamentarian estates. Parliament's war aims were more complicated. Many, like Rudyerd, who was still at Westminster, were deeply unhappy about being in arms against the king at all. It was dangerous – they were guilty of treason – and it went against deep-seated principles of loyalty and duty. They hoped that, if they could avoid defeat, the king could be brought to negotiate. Many believed that, in the words of Nathaniel Fiennes MP, they were 'fighting to maintain the laws and true religion', not 'fighting against the law to overthrow one government thereby established and set up another'. 'We need not, we will not, he went on, 'to gain a peace be without a king, no nor without this king: only he himself hath brought this necessity upon us, not to trust him with that power whereby he may do us and himself hurt.'[3] The settlement they envisaged would be based on the legislation of 1641, with the addition that the king would share with Parliament his choice of ministers and power over the armed forces. They also expected the punishment of at least some of the most active 'delinquents'. They disliked the idea of all-out war and could not see what total victory could achieve: hardly anyone conceived of a regime that was not based on monarchy. They assumed that the king would continue to govern and that any settlement would have to include him. Others shared these basic objectives, but differed as to how they could be achieved. They did not believe that Charles could be brought to make concessions while hostilities were still going on; it would be necessary to defeat him militarily and then impose conditions on him. It did not occur to anybody that he might refuse to make concessions even after he had been comprehensively defeated.

The hesitancy and unease of many Parliamentarians helps explain their conduct in the first year of the war. Their aim was to avoid defeat. Parliament voted no taxes for the war, relying on loans and gifts. The Act encouraging 'adventurers' to invest in the reconquest of Ireland promised confiscated land in return for advances of money; these funds were raided to help pay for the war effort in England. In the early months both sides consolidated and extended their control of their respective territories. The one significant battle was at Edgehill, Warwickshire, on 23 October. Essex's army was well equipped and raised mainly in and around London. The king's was a motley set of units, many raised by individual gentlemen, including a significant number of Welshmen. Many Royalists believed that in the final analysis Parliamentarian soldiers would not fight against their king. Parliament was confident that its forces were superior, so the battle proved something of a shock. The Royalist cavalry under Rupert cut through Essex's cavalry and proceeded to plunder the baggage train. The infantry on both sides fought until they were exhausted; the Royalist infantry were probably saved from defeat by the return to the field of Rupert's cavalry. The Parliamentarians withdrew from the field the following morning. Casualties were about even on both sides, but the Parliamentarians had failed to halt the Royalist advance towards London. In November the king's forces advanced as far as Brentford, which they sacked. Fearfully, the London militia marched

towards them, determined to defend their homes. They met at
Turnham Green, a few miles west of Hammersmith. Rather
than risk a battle, the king's forces retreated to Oxford, which
became the Royalists' capital, for the winter. This was the
nearest the Royalists came to an assault on London, which in
1643 was to be surrounded by earthworks, eighteen feet high,
constructed by the citizens and their wives and children.

The war went no better for Parliament in 1643. The king
planned an ambitious three-pronged assault from the North,
the West Midlands and the South-west. The Parliamentarians
were defeated at Roundway Down in Wiltshire and Adwalton
Moor in Yorkshire; the latter left Parliament's position in the
North very precarious. In July, amid accusations of treachery,
the key port of Bristol fell to the king. Essex, of whom so much
had been expected, proved a less than dynamic general;
complaints about him mounted. To make matters worse the
king had the prospect of assistance from Ireland. Since the
rising of 1641 the Catholics of Ireland had organized themselves in the Confederation of Kilkenny. In 1642–3 there had
been an inconclusive conflict between the Confederates and
the Irish Protestant Royalists, led by the marquis of Ormond.
In September 1643 they agreed a truce which freed many of the
Protestant forces to come to the assistance of the king. Tension
was high in London and at Westminster. Some blamed the
defeats on treachery; a few had actually defected to the king,
while others seemed lukewarm towards the Parliamentary
cause or sceptical of the possibility of victory. As the king
showed no inclination to come to terms, the only options
seemed to be a slow apathetic slide towards defeat, or a greatly
invigorated war effort.

After much debate, Parliament opted for the latter. Both sides
had been wooing the Scots since before the war started, but
Parliament now increased its offer and its suit was successful.
Since 1641 the clergy had gained ground within the
Covenanting movement at the expense of the nobility, and the
clergy remained committed to the hope of bringing the English

Church into line with that of Scotland. The king, with his commitment to bishops, could not agree to this. Many in Parliament disliked some aspects of Scottish Presbyterianism, especially the power that the clergy wielded over the laity, and the claim that theirs was the only divinely approved model of church government; but they were prepared to swallow their scruples if it meant winning Scottish military support. The Solemn League and Covenant, concluded in September, committed the Scots to supply 20,000 men, paid for in substantial part by Parliament. In return, those Englishmen who subscribed to the Covenant promised to reform the Churches of England and Ireland, 'in doctrine, worship, discipline and government, according to the Word of God and the example of the best reformed churches'.[4] It is difficult to see this as anything other than a cynical fudge. The Scots were in no doubt that theirs was one of the best Reformed churches, but the wording did not commit those taking the Covenant unequivocally to making the English Church exactly like that of Scotland.

The Scottish alliance brought a welcome injection of experienced and well-motivated soldiers into the Parliamentary war effort. A similar injection of energy and zeal was needed in the organization and financing of the war. In most regions there was great reluctance to use the militia for anything other than local defence. Only in East Anglia and Cambridgeshire did the earl of Manchester and Oliver Cromwell succeed in creating an effective association, with its own administration and treasury. The Eastern Association, indeed, showed that it was possible to create an effective army based on the county militias, but elsewhere attempts to do so were defeated by localism and obstruction; counties sent to the armies those men who could best be spared – petty criminals and unemployables. It was difficult to transmit to the localities an urgent sense that the war needed to be won. The task of doing so was entrusted to local committees, mostly county-based. Whereas pre-war justices of the peace had been chosen in part because of their social rank and standing in the county, committee men were chosen because of their commitment to the war. Some were indeed members of major county families, such as Sir Thomas Pelham and Herbert Morley in Sussex. Others were men of rank, but outsiders, such as the splenetic Sir Anthony Weldon in Kent. Others again were of much humbler status, the sort of men who would never have aspired to senior county rank before the civil war, and who owed their elevation to their zeal for the cause. One of the most spectacular examples of these was John Pyne, an attorney of obscure birth, who emerged as the 'county boss' of Somerset. Overall, the county committees took over responsibility for the war effort in the localities, leaving the old authorities, headed by the justices of the peace, responsible for the civil government, at least in theory. In practice, the exigencies of the war effort meant that the committees frequently trespassed on the preserve of the magistrates, issued orders to civilian officers and overruled their superiors.[5]

The multiplicity of committees in the localities had their counterparts at the centre. Even before the war, the untrustworthiness and negligence of the king had driven the Houses to appoint committees to perform executive functions, such as providing for national defence in his absence. Using committees came naturally to the Houses. While the Commons or the Lords as a whole decided on the broad outlines and principles of the bills that might become laws, a smaller body was needed to do the detailed work of drafting. As a rule those nominated to these committees were members with a particular interest in the bill: godly Puritans for bills about sabbath observance, merchants or MPs representing major ports for bills on trade, and so on. Under the Tudors the Commons also appointed committees with a wider remit, to gather information on grievances or religion, for example. In 1621 when the Commons wanted to investigate monopolies and other financial scams linked to the king's government, they set up a committee to investigate. A committee formed a body of a practical size to absorb complex data and make decisions about gathering revenue or transmitting money to army units

in the field. As committees consisted of members of both
Houses, they formed a valuable link between them. Some also
included men who were not members of Parliament, notably
London businessmen: indeed the committee for taking the
accounts of the kingdom included no member of either House.
There tended to be an overlap of membership between
committees, which again provided an element of cohesion.
Those who attended regularly tended to be relatively few in
number. When MPs had been elected back in 1640, they had
expected the Parliament to last at most a few months. They had
not expected that they would have to face the expense and
trouble of having to live in London for years at a time, or
handling heavy administrative responsibilities of a sort that no
Parliament had handled before. Some of the more arithmeti-
cally challenged found the numbers difficult. Others missed
their homes and their neighbours; if they lived in Royalist areas
or war zones, they might fear attack and plunder. And some
who were genuinely zealous for the war effort felt that they
might be more useful if they were with the armies rather than
at Westminster.

As the committees were relatively small and contained many
who were eager in their support for the war, those who
favoured a more aggressive approach found them easier to
manage than the House of Commons as a whole. There many
MPs remained wedded to ideals of compromise and consensus
which were not compatible with fighting a vigorous and
effective war. Debates could drag on, decisions were delayed,
and the House's mood could be capricious and unpredictable.
Those with firm policy objectives needed to manage the
Houses, but they could get much done in the committees,
which increasingly operated outside the knowledge of the
Commons as a whole. By 1643 there were two distinct groups
among these political leaders. On one hand were those led by
the earl of Northumberland and Denzil Holles, one of the five
members. They preferred a strategy of limited military action,
which meant limited taxation and limited interference in

civilian life, and a quick negotiated peace with the king. On the other side there were a group of peers headed initially by Essex and Manchester and by the quaintly named Lord Saye and Sele, and (until his untimely death in 1643) John Pym. (Another leader, John Hampden, was killed in 1642).[6] These believed that the war had to be won and everything else had to be subordinated to that end. Parliament had to overcome its aversion to raising taxes without the king and its respect for the legal rights of subjects. Unless Parliament did everything it could to raise men and money, together with horses, munitions and provisions for the armies, Parliament risked defeat and a royal tyranny far worse than anything England had experienced in the 1630s.

In order to make war as effectively as possible, Parliament needed a body that could coordinate the work of the various committees and think strategically. That body was at first the committee of safety, which gradually accumulated more powers. Although its power in some areas was undermined by the creation of new specialist committees, its own remit was sufficiently vague for it to intervene in areas controlled by other bodies. (In general, it is extremely difficult to define the precise responsibilities of any of the major committees, such as those for the army and navy, because they kept changing and often overstepped their limits, while fending off attempts by other bodies to interfere within what they saw as their patch.) Initially Parliament, perhaps displaying its traditional suspicion of the possible misuse of power, dispersed authority between committees, which made coordination difficult. What is clear is that the political leaders vied for control of the key committees, such as that for the army, and above all the committee of safety. After the signing of the Solemn League and Covenant, the latter was superseded by the committee for both kingdoms, which contained Scots as well as English. Its task was to 'advise, consult, order and direct, concerning the carrying on and managing the war for the best advantage'.[7] To the outrage of many in Parliament, its members had to take an oath to keep its proceedings secret. It soon became apparent that it considered itself independent of the Parliament which had created it – for example, carrying on negotiations with the king. However, it lacked direct authority over the commanders-in-chief of the English and Scottish armies, the earl of Essex and Alexander Leslie, since 1641 earl of Leven, who were also independent of one another.

If Parliament was to stand any chance of winning an outright victory, it would have to increase dramatically the resources devoted to the war, and that meant raising more money; for a start it was committed to paying £30,000 a month towards the Scottish army's maintenance. To make matters worse, the reforming legislation of 1641 had swept away many of the revenues of the monarchy. Kings traditionally derived much of their income from their own estates, from vestiges of the feudal powers of the medieval monarchy, or from their position as king (for example, fines in the law courts). The income from crown lands had been drastically reduced by repeated sales and most of the feudal sources of revenue had been abolished in 1641. None of these personal sources of royal revenue could be seen as taxes: sums levied on specific forms of income or property, or on commodities, at standard fixed rates. The only taxes collected legitimately by the crown before 1640 were those voted by Parliament. These consisted of tonnage and poundage, import duties, voted to most kings for life at the start of their reign, and taxes on land, voted to meet the costs of war. Import duties fell mainly on luxuries, above all wine and brandy, and so were paid only by a narrow, wealthy segment of the population. Tudor Parliaments introduced a new land tax called the subsidy. Under each subsidy act, commissioners were appointed for each county who were to receive statements of income from landowners, and then fix the amount each was to pay on the basis of their declared income. Landowners were allowed to deduct 'necessary' expenses; as they were not on oath, they could be creative, if not downright fraudulent, in the figures they returned. Lord

Burghley, Elizabeth's lord treasurer, returned his landed income as £133 a year – on which he managed to build Burghley House. The only check was that they needed the approval of the commissioners, who were often their friends and neighbours. Moreover, as those appointed as commissioners were not always the same, those who dealt kindly with their neighbours on one occasion could expect the same if their roles were reversed on another.

All in all, this was not a fiscal system designed to raise large sums of money quickly and efficiently. The import duties were paid by a smallish minority, which overlapped to some extent with those liable to pay feudal dues to the king. Evasion of the subsidy had become so widespread that by the late 1620s a single subsidy yielded less than half the sum produced under Elizabeth – and this despite the fact that there had been severe price inflation in the interim. The Commons tried to get round this by voting two, four or even six subsidies; taxpayers responded by under-assessing their income even more grossly. Charles I's financial advisers had been well aware of this and had tried to tackle the problem when collecting ship money, using a system that was used in collecting a variety of local rates. Instead of assessing each landowner individually, each county, or part of a county, was given a quota to meet, which was apportioned between the taxpayers. Thus if one person paid less, another would have to pay more. At first many complained that they were overrated, but soon the apportionments became fixed and ship money was collected exceptionally efficiently by seventeenth-century standards, with yields nationwide generally running above 90 per cent of the quotas. This approach to assessment had obvious attractions to a Parliament that needed to raise large sums quickly. Parliament authorized a 'weekly collection' in the spring of 1643 and this became the monthly assessment, raised at many times the rate of ship money. The money raised was designated specifically to pay the armies.

Effective as it became, the monthly assessment taxed only one kind of property. The only commodities on which taxes were collected were those liable to tonnage and poundage. Other, vast areas of economic activity, remained untaxed, but not for long. The Dutch, in their long war of liberation against Spain, had had to find ways of raising very large sums of money from a small population. They had come up with the excise: a tax on commodities produced and sold within the country (although it could easily be extended to cover imports as well). It had the additional advantage that, once the general principle had been accepted, it could be extended to more and more commodities. The excise duties introduced by Parliament in 1643 fell on a wide range of goods, but later the list was reduced. The meat and salt excises were abandoned after violent resistance, notably a riot at Smithfield meat market in London in 1647. It became apparent that it was unwise to try to collect the meat excise in the market place, where the butchers' stalls were all together in the 'shambles' – butchers had knives and cleavers and a reputation for violence. In time, the excise came to be levied mainly on alcoholic drinks – beer, cider and perry. Although many were too poor to eat meat regularly, beer was part of the staple diet of men, women and children: water was not safe to drink and tea and coffee, although known, were expensive luxuries. The beer excise, in particular, brought the poor suddenly and brutally into the tax system. Small wonder there was resistance. It soon became apparent that it was safer to collect the beer excise from the brewers rather than in the alehouses, where drunken customers were liable to attack the collectors.

The introduction of these new excises showed that Parliament now put raising money before maintaining the goodwill of the people. Already its local agents had shown a growing ruthlessness. Estates were confiscated from 'delinquents' on flimsy evidence. Even where the victim's Royalism was unquestionable, sequestration could lead to an ugly outbreak of asset stripping and downright theft as Parliament's agents 'valued' the property. Later those whose estates had been sequestered were allowed to 'compound' for them – in other words, buy them back. How much they paid depended on perceptions of the gravity of their 'delinquency' – and on who their friends were. Parliament also introduced the 'fifth and twentieth part'. Those who had not lent money voluntarily to Parliament in 1642 were now required to pay one-fifth of their annual income and one-twentieth of the value of their goods, as assessed by a local Parliamentary committee; again the opportunities for favouritism, victimization, extortion and theft were legion. The excisemen should have operated according to fixed rules, but it became apparent that some brewers could negotiate more favourable deals than others. Moreover, the excisemen's rights of search seemed limitless: they could search the premises of 'every person that selleth, buyeth or spendeth any of the said commodities'.[8] In 1640–2 Parliament had complained endlessly about the king's failure to respect the rule of law. From 1643 Parliament flouted the rule of law far more consistently and shamelessly than the king ever had. Lord Wharton told the Lords 'they were not tied to a law, for these were times of necessity and imminent danger'.[9] Its ruthless methods were to enable it to win the war – but at huge political cost.

The new ruthlessness which Parliament brought to the war in 1643 was not matched by the Royalists. In statements such as his answer to the Nineteen Propositions, Charles had taken his stand on the ancient constitution and the rule of law. In the early stages of the war his commanders had been encouraged to seek the cooperation and consent of local rulers wherever possible. The commitment to the rule of law was reinforced when Charles summoned a Royalist Parliament, consisting of members of both Houses who had come over to him; it assembled at Oxford in January 1644. The majority of members expected the king to respect the ancient constitution. Although it agreed to 'vote' the king taxes in the areas he controlled, it did so more hesitantly, indeed reluctantly, than its counterpart at Westminster. Charles became increasingly impatient with the members, who kept badgering him to come to terms with

Parliament. He accused it of being a 'mongrel Parliament', producing 'base and mutinous motions'. He adjourned it in March 1645 and never summoned it again.[10] Parliament already enjoyed a substantial advantage from its possession of London, which increased as the gap between the resources available to the two sides began to grow. But resources, crucial though they were, could not alone guarantee victory. Parliament also needed to begin to defeat the king's armies.

The arrival of the Scottish army in the North at once transformed the balance of power there. It would no longer be possible to send a substantial Northern army to take part in an attack on London. The North was also, with Wales, one of the Royalists' main recruiting grounds. In July 1644 Parliament gained control of Newcastle, and with it London's supply of coal, and threatened York, the Royalists' capital in the North. Rupert hurried north to relieve the city, but before he could reach it he was intercepted at Marston Moor. Although on one flank the Royalist cavalry drove the Parliamentarians back, on the other Rupert was routed by cavalry commanded by Cromwell and the Scot David Leslie. In the centre the infantry fought fiercely until Cromwell attacked the Royalists from the rear. Parliament lost about 1,500 men, the Royalists between 3,000 and 4,000. This was their first major defeat, and with it they lost York and the North. It was a huge psychological blow, and Parliament expected that the war would soon be over. But it was not to be. Parliament's armies were in an appalling state. Sick, and exhausted, the soldiers lacked shoes and clothes. The Eastern Association counties claimed that they were no longer able to bear the cost of the armies. This helps to explain why Essex failed to follow up the advantage that had been gained. Instead, he was driven through Devon and Cornwall and forced into a humiliating surrender at Lostwithiel on 21 August. He did not improve his reputation by fighting another drawn battle at Newbury. The Royalists regrouped and their confidence returned. On the Parliamentarian side there were complaints, hints of treachery, and suggestions that some did not really want victory. Cromwell fell out with his former patron and ally, the earl of Manchester, who was discredited in the eyes of many by his mishandling of the second battle of Newbury. Manchester was alleged to have said that if they defeated the king ninety-nine times he would still be king. Cromwell asked why, in that case, they had ever taken up arms against him, but Manchester had already given the answer in his next sentence: if the king defeated them just once, their lives would be forfeit and their descendants made slaves.[11] Even so, there was a difference of emphasis: Cromwell believed much could be gained from victory, Manchester only that they must not risk defeat; he also accused Cromwell of favouring sectaries. In the mood prevailing in Parliament in the latter part of 1644 Manchester's attitude smacked of defeatism, which could serve only to prolong the war.

In November the Commons considered the Parliamentary armies' signal lack of success after Marston Moor and their problems of leadership, resources and morale. As far as leadership was concerned, the key figure was not Manchester but Essex. Parliament had appointed him commander-in-chief of the English army and militia, and entrusted him with directing the military side of the war effort. Although some would have liked simply to dismiss him, to do so would have alienated the Lords; those who remained at Westminster were not numerous, and it was essential to keep them there to maintain the claim that this was indeed a Parliament, not just a House of Commons. If Essex was to be eased out, it would have to be done in a way that allowed him to save face and avoided alienating the rest of the peers. The Saye group, whose leader in the Commons since Pym's death was Oliver St John, argued that the failure to follow up Marston Moor reflected the righteous judgement of God. The Parliamentarians were being punished for their sins; to appease the wrath of God a collective act of self-sacrifice was required. Those officers in the army (and holders of major civilian offices) who were also members of either House should resign their commissions. This would enable them to devote more time to the business of Parliament, which was suffering from falling attendances, and allow new officers to be appointed who were committed solely to the army and could be expected to carry on the war with the utmost vigour. The thinking behind this Self-Denying Ordinance was one normally associated with the godly, who saw God's providence at work everywhere, but there was to be no distinction among those removed between the godly and the rest: Cromwell was to resign as well as Essex, although a way was soon found for Cromwell to resume his command. The ordinance was followed by the creation of a New Model Army out of the existing armies, particularly that of the Eastern Association. This was intended to be a national army, free from the localism that had hampered some of the existing armies. Although many of the officers had served in the Eastern Association army, its commander-in-chief, Sir Thomas Fairfax, was from Yorkshire. Officers were to be appointed and promoted on the basis of talent and experience, rather than birth. Care was taken in drawing up the lists of officers for each regiment. Although these contained officers of various political and religious persuasions, and the rank and file included many former Royalists, the opposition shown by the Lords to many of those who were nominated would suggest that they were seen as more radical, in religion and politics, than officers in most of the existing armies.[12]

The formation of the New Model was the military equivalent of the introduction of the monthly assessment and the excise in the drive for outright victory. Cromwell was convinced that much of the success of the Eastern Association army, above all at Marston Moor, derived from the commitment of the soldiers, and especially the cavalry. The cavalry was the elite wing of the army, volunteers rather than conscripts, and of sufficient means to provide their own horses. As Cromwell later explained, most of the original Parliamentarian cavalry were 'old decayed serving men and tapsters and such kind of fellows', who were routed by the 'gentlemen's sons' in the Royalist cavalry; perhaps he was thinking of Edgehill. Cromwell, a gentleman himself, believed that men of gentle birth were normally more effective in battle, having the qualities of courage and a well-developed sense of honour. (On the other hand, some gentlemen officers seemed incapable of obeying orders, while some units would obey only the gentleman who had recruited them.) To defeat them other martial qualities were needed, and his men brought a commitment to the Parliamentary cause and godly zeal: 'men of a spirit that is likely to go as far as a gentleman will go'.[13] They believed in what they were fighting for, as set out in Parliament's declarations, and had volunteered to fight for it. They also read and discussed the news and other products of the press, especially in the long days of inactivity in winter quarters. Their godly zeal gave them a conviction that God was guiding them and that they would be victorious: they were a godly remnant, a 'handful of despised men', an army of saints, separate and different from civilian society and the ways of the world. They saw themselves as 'strangers and pilgrims here' in the world, an attitude which gave them a 'holy ruthlessness'.[14] Some regiments, but by no means all, resembled gathered churches. Both officers and soldiers addressed prayer meetings, despite repeated prohibitions of lay preaching by Parliament. Later, when the army was considering a decisive move, a prayer meeting would be called so that they could steel themselves for action.

The New Model's superior motivation and morale was matched by strict discipline. Drunkenness and looting were not tolerated, with the result that this army generally encountered less civilian hostility than other armies. Its officers, under the overall command of Sir Thomas Fairfax, were generally careful to treat the civilian authorities with tact and respect, but also there was a strong solidarity between officers and men, born of mutual trust and respect. In all this it helped that the Saye–St John group and their allies in Parliament and on the key committees ensured that the New Model was paid more regularly than the other armies, which at times were starved of money, leading to indiscipline and free quarter. When the Saye–St John group, and many of the Northern MPs, turned against the Scots, they became the worst paid of all, and the worst behaved; they were, of course, fighting in a foreign country. By now many believed that the Scots were a political liability and militarily useless: there were even proposals that the New Model should drive them back to Scotland.[15] The New Model, on the other hand, was given the lion's share of resources because it was expected to bring victory on the battlefield. This came in June.

A revolt led by the marquis of Montrose was seriously embarrassing the Covenanting regime. Charles hoped that if his army could link up with Montrose, they could secure Scotland and then sweep down into England. His army was intercepted by the New Model at Naseby in Northamptonshire. Although the Royalists were substantially inferior in numbers, they insisted on charging the enemy uphill. As at Edgehill, Rupert's cavalry broke through on one flank, but then rode off to plunder the baggage train. The fighting on the other flank was much more even, until the Royalists' courage failed them and they fled. About 500 were killed and 5,000 taken prisoner. To make matters worse the king's papers were seized, including some relating to his dealings with the Confederate Catholics in Ireland; these were quickly published under the title *The King's Cabinet Opened*. Other intercepted letters were to show the king (and queen) seeking military help from the prince of Orange, Denmark, France, Scotland and Ireland (again) and financial help from the assembly of the French Catholic clergy and the pope.[16] Soon after Montrose was defeated at Philiphaugh and all hope of relief from Scotland ended. The assistance hoped for from Ireland, bought by ever more extravagant concessions to the Confederates, never materialized.

In the aftermath of Naseby the amount of territory controlled by the Royalists shrank. Rupert urged the king to negotiate: 'I believe it a more prudent way to retain something than to lose all.' Charles's response was uncompromising: 'God will not suffer rebels and traitors to prosper or this cause to be overthrown'; he was prepared 'to die for a good cause'.[17] When Bristol fell to Parliament in August, the king blamed Rupert, who had told him bluntly that it could not be defended. Charles dismissed him from his service and ordered him to leave the country; in fact he did not.[18] In order to keep the war going, local commanders abandoned the attempt to work with the local rulers and squeezed as much as they could out of the people. The outcome was popular resistance to the soldiery, even in ultra-loyal South Wales. There was similar resistance to the exactions of the Parliamentary armies over much of south and south-west England, but Parliament was winning the war, taxes were being collected, and many Parliamentary commanders tried to appease civilian anger; if they did decide to use force, however, civilian resistance quickly crumbled. The winter of 1645–6 saw the Royalists being driven back and back. A symbol of Parliament's extended control was that the Commons began in August 1645 to hold 'recruiter' elections, to fill vacancies created by deaths and the expulsion of Royalist MPs from constituencies in what had been Royalist areas. By the spring of 1646 it was largely a matter of mopping up. The king sent his eldest son, Charles, abroad. In June Oxford surrendered to Fairfax and the king surrendered his person to the Scots.

Parliament had won the war, for a number of reasons. The fact it was based in London helped, and not just because of the huge resources in terms of men and money there. London was also the capital city and Parliament's remaining at Westminster emphasized its authority and legitimacy as an institution. Despite the departure of some members to the king, and the expulsion of others, it was still an elected body – and vacancies began to be filled by election – and could claim to represent the people. The continued presence of the Lords, albeit in smallish numbers, added to that sense of legitimacy and continuity. This was most crucially important in securing obedience to its ordinances, even though they did not have the assent of the king, especially those imposing unprecedented level of taxation. The English were accustomed to obey laws passed by Parliament, and pay taxes voted by Parliament, and they did so now, despite myriad grumbles and widespread protests. It also helped the Parliamentary cause that Parliament controlled the navy and that it was able to secure military help from Scotland at a crucial time, however much it later undervalued that help. Charles, on the other hand, failed to secure any significant military assistance from Ireland and suffered enormous political damage when it became known how great were the concessions he had been prepared to offer the Confederate Catholics. He was also an indecisive leader, prone to bouts of pessimism and gloom. Parliament, though, had won the key battles, albeit helped at times, notably at Naseby, by serious errors on the part of the Royalist commanders. But above all, Parliament had overcome its initial reticence, indeed embarrassment, about being at war with the king, and fought with determination and even ruthlessness. The monthly assessment and the excise, and a multitude of local financial levies, provided the money. The alliance with the Scots – never loved, often hated – showed a new determination to enlarge the armies; the creation of the New Model gave Parliament an army with the fighting qualities needed to defeat the Royalists. But victory came at a price.

The popular support which Parliament had enjoyed in 1642–3 had largely evaporated by early 1646. The people were weary of the war, war taxation and the depredations of soldiers. The means used by Parliament to win the war seemed, to many, far more oppressive than those used by the king in the 1630s. There was talk of Parliamentary tyranny; Parliament was seen as a body bloated and corrupted by power, whose agents grew rich while taxpayers struggled to survive.[19] The 'Clubmen' who appeared in many counties in 1644–6 called for a return to normal, with reduced taxation and no soldiers; and to many of them, the least bad way of achieving this seemed to be an almost unconditional restoration of the king's power. It could be predicted early in 1646 that Parliament would find it difficult to satisfy popular aspirations for a speedy return to normal while negotiating a settlement with the king which could guard against another Personal Rule. But within a year of the king's surrender to the Scots, something much more unpredictable and extraordinary was to happen: like Frankenstein's monster the New Model was to turn against the Parliament that had created it.

6

THE WAR AND THE PEOPLE

The impact of the first civil war on the people of England and Wales was unprecedented and traumatic. The most recent civil wars, the Wars of the Roses, had involved a relatively small number of noblemen and their followings, and most battles had been on a modest scale. In 1642–6 a quarter or even a third of the adult male population may have been in arms at some time, and one in ten at any given time. The war affected ordinary men and women throughout the country. The few areas that saw little or no fighting were those under the more or less undisputed control of one side or the other. Parliament controlled much of the south-east: East Anglia, Kent and East Sussex, Hertfordshire and Cambridgeshire; London and Middlesex saw no hostilities after the Royalist retreat from Turnham Green in 1642. Royalist control, except in large parts of Wales, was never so complete, because there were Parliamentarian enclaves in the areas of initial Royalist dominance: the south-west, the West Midlands and the North. But even the areas which saw little or no fighting were deeply affected by the war, as the demands of both sides for men and money became ever heavier. Moreover, Parliament's punitive measures against Royalists, Catholics and Laudians, attacks on traditional parish worship and heavy-handed attempts at moral reform, constituted a form of ideological warfare and proved deeply divisive and destructive. Those areas which were contested throughout the war – large parts of the Midlands, central southern and south-western England (with the partial exception of Cornwall) – saw the heaviest demands for men and money and suffered the highest levels of war damage, economic disruption, military violence and plunder. In such contested areas, many military commanders saw destruction and plunder as necessary to cow a disaffected population. But even a county like Hertfordshire, where any threat from the Royalists had been snuffed out before the end of 1642, saw significant levels of plunder and wanton damage by the soldiery.

There was no standing army in England in 1642. The nearest thing to a permanent military force was the militia, in which civilians were given some basic military training. Its function was seen essentially as local defence: in wartime it watched the coasts and prepared beacons to warn those inland in case of invasion. It also rounded up those seen as potentially disaffected – Catholics at the time of the Armada, for example. With the possible exception of that of London, the militia would be no match for experienced, battle-hardened soldiers. In addition, it could not be required to serve outside the country – indeed, some claimed it could not be ordered out of the county in which it was raised. For this reason, for foreign expeditions – including those planned against Scotland in 1639–40 – the king also ordered the raising of units of pressed men, conscripts, selected from among those members of society who could be most easily spared. The performance of such men in the Cadiz and La Rochelle expeditions of the 1620s, or at Newburn in 1640, did not inspire confidence in their military competence. In 1642 Parliament secured control of the militia and set out to place it in reliable hands, removing those seen as Royalist sympathizers. It also encouraged the raising of volunteer units among its more committed supporters. The king, lacking the machinery of the militia, also encouraged volunteers, and issued commissions to men whom he regarded as loyal and of sufficient rank to attract officers and men to serve under them. Both sides, but especially the Royalists, were strengthened by the return home of soldiers of fortune who had served in continental armies, and these were joined by experienced foreign soldiers, including many Scots.

Personal loyalty to the king gave a direction and impetus to the Royalist cause which many of the Parliamentary forces lacked. Much of the militia, and many of those who commanded it, saw local defence as their primary concern, and showed little interest in the wider conflict. In an attempt to overcome this localism, Parliament grouped counties into regional associations, but only in the eastern counties (Norfolk, Suffolk, Essex, Cambridgeshire and Hertfordshire) was an effective regional organization established. Throughout the areas under Parliament's control, including the Eastern Association, the county, traditionally the basic unit of local administration, became the basis for the organization of the war effort. As it became apparent that those who traditionally directed county government (the justices of the peace) and the militia (the lord lieutenant and deputy lieutenants) lacked sufficient zeal for the war effort, Parliament created new bodies, county committees, to direct operations. (The king, by contrast, tried to work with the traditional county authorities and to win a measure of consent for the raising of men and money.) The nature and powers of county committees varied greatly. In some counties, there were one or two dominant committees, in others several, often with overlapping membership, but there were also bodies, notably accounts sub-committees, which saw their role as checking on, and curbing, the county committees. The county committees did not take kindly to such supervision. They harassed the members of sub-committees, starting lawsuits against them, over-assessing them for taxation and committing them to gaol.[1] In some counties the traditional authorities tried to reassert themselves. Grand juries, perhaps the most authentic voice of county opinion, demanded that power be handed back to the traditional authorities, and occasionally, as in Hertfordshire in 1644, Parliament was persuaded to hand power over the militia back to the lieutenancy, to the fury of the county's militia committee. Parliament soon changed its mind. The general trend was for power to become concentrated in the county committees, and normal county government, even in areas not touched by the fighting, was increasingly interrupted or ceased altogether. In Warwickshire, where there was extensive fighting, no quarter sessions were held between September 1642 and 1645.[2]

Whereas the traditional offices had been filled by members of the leading landed families, most committees were staffed by men of humbler origins – lesser gentry, lawyers, townsmen – who were zealous for the Parliamentary cause. (Grand juries often complained of the low status of county committeemen.) Their confidence in the righteousness of their cause made them ruthless. They saw neutralism and moderation as evidence of Royalism, and divided people into good Parliamentarians, or the godly, and 'malignants' or 'delinquents'. The committee of Kent demanded that those they saw as malignants should pay additional taxation.[3] Landowners whose support for Parliament was less than wholehearted were condemned as covert Royalists and their property was arbitrarily confiscated. Those accused of disobeying the committees' orders were imprisoned, without due process of law, even though it was doubtful whether they had any lawful authority to commit people to gaol. Their proceedings, unlike those of the law courts, were secret: in the words of that most moderate of MPs, Sir John Holland, 'they will judge by no other rule that that of their own wills and those judgements shall be sure to be put in execution with all manner of rigour'.[4] Their feuds were some-times so bitter that they were accused of violence and even torture against their supposed colleagues.[5] The situation was not helped by administrative confusion. New institutions of local administration were put together piecemeal by Parliamentary ordinances which were rushed through with little consideration of whether they were consistent with one another. The confusions and anomalies that this created allowed committees to proceed with an arrogant disregard for the rule of law, safe in the knowledge that the only recourse of their victims was to appeal to a House of Commons in which many MPs believed that those who were not wholeheartedly with Parliament were against it.

As the war progressed, and the scale of operations increased, the flow of volunteers dried up. The militia, normally seen as an occasional force, became permanent, and militiamen became, with experience, competent soldiers. Both sides increasingly had recourse to impressment. All these soldiers had to be paid. Initially Parliament was reluctant to vote taxes, and instead invited its supporters to give or lend money (or horses or other support in kind) in response to 'the propositions'. By early 1643, it was apparent that this would not produce enough for that year's war effort; some counties were already raising money for their forces, over and above the militia rate. Parliament therefore introduced the weekly assessment, a tax mainly on land, similar to ship money, but at a much higher rate. It also ordered a tax on the real and personal property of those who had not contributed voluntarily on the propositions, and the sequestration of the property of 'malignants', which was to be managed to raise money for the war effort. As time went on, more and more new taxes were added. Landowners in Hertfordshire had to pay taxes for the county's own forces, many of whom were serving outside the county; a substantial contribution to the Eastern Association and the garrison of Newport Pagnell; fortifications for the major towns; and (perhaps most resented of all) towards the maintenance of the Scottish army. To this was added the new burden of the excise, which fell upon everyone, although as the machinery took time to establish, its full weight was not felt until after the end of the war. However, there was violent opposition to excise collectors from at least 1644. The multiplicity of taxes, and the variety of bodies handling the money, makes the overall burden impossible to calculate, but it has been estimated that in Norfolk in the late 1640s the assessment alone brought in ten times the yield of the Parliamentary taxation of the 1620s, and the excise more than twice as much.[6] Similarly, Kent in 1645–6 was required to pay more than twelve times as much for the assessment as it had paid for ship money.[7]

But the taxes were only part of the burden. The demand from the armies for horses, carts and provisions seemed never-ending. Horses were taken from the plough, and from the carts in harvest-time, leaving farmers unable to sow or to reap; there were also complaints of shortages of manpower on the farms, making it impossible to gather in the harvest. Some land went untilled, many tenant farmers were barely able to make ends meet and rents remained unpaid. While some manufacturers and craftsmen profited from the needs of the armies for clothing and boots, weapons and armour, many more had their liveli-hoods disrupted, as military operations, especially sieges, inter-rupted trade. And on top of everything else there was the burden of the soldiers. Despite the best efforts of the county committees, not enough money was collected to meet the seem-ingly insatiable demands of the armies; even the most diligent were forced to borrow. There was a constant shortage of ready cash, and the soldiers' pay was usually in arrears. In 1644 the Eastern Association cavalry received pay for 126 days, Essex's army for 98 and Sir William Waller's army for 77.[8] Soldiers had no money to replace worn-out clothing and shoes, so stole them from civilians or stripped corpses. They had no choice but to have recourse to free quarter. Soldiers were billeted on civilians, who were to provide them with food and lodging and (even more burdensome) stabling and forage for the horses of the cavalry. In theory, soldiers were expected to pay or, if they had no money, to give their reluctant hosts tickets setting out what they were owed, which would (also in theory) be redeemed by the Parliamentarian authorities later. In practice, many soldiers failed or refused to give tickets, and many who received them were unable to have them honoured. Those forced to receive Royalist soldiers in the latter stages of the war were even less likely to be reimbursed. Soldiers moved slowly, often in small groups and without officers, and might choose to stay in one place for several days. The problem of free quarter was worst in the winter, when it was impossible to house the troops under canvas, and large bodies of men were quartered on small communities. (In summer, only officers had tents: the men slept in the open or in billets.) To make matters worse, the soldiers in winter had little to do and were bored; friction with civilians, and plundering, became increasingly likely.

The scale of free quarter was enormous: it has been suggested that it cost the people more than was raised in taxation.[9] But the impact of the armies went wider. Garrison commanders exacted contributions of money, horses and provisions from the surrounding countryside. Soldiers in garrisons were often unsupervised and could degenerate into little more than bandits, threatening to burn people's homes if their demands for 'contributions' were not met. At Malmesbury in 1645 the people complained that they provided free quarter and draft horses for the Parliamentarian garrison, which spent its time drinking. At the same time the Royalists also demanded contributions and plundered the county, and the garrison did nothing to protect them.[10] The commander of the garrison at Compton House, Warwickshire, ordered local villagers to work without pay on the fortifications there, and made it clear that this was a punishment for their alleged Royalism. He sent the order 'to the most base malignant constable and towns of Tysoe [etc] . . . upon pain of imprisonment and plundering'.[11] Purchasing supplies or making tax assessments could shade into seizure, which in turn could degenerate into plunder; which of these it really was could be in the eye of the beholder. The Worcestershire county committee told the villagers of Elmley Lovett to pay what was demanded of them within three days: 'you will answer the contrary at your peril of pillaging and plundering, and your houses fired and your persons imprisoned'.[12] Although the king's stated policy was to seek civilian consent, individual commanders were using threats and violence to collect money as early as the spring of 1643.[13] The word 'plunder', indeed, was first used in English in 1642.[14]

Unpaid soldiers held mayors, aldermen or the members of county committees to ransom, forcing them to hand over money for their pay. For ordinary soldiers the temptation to plunder civilians was often irresistible: their weapons gave them power. Civilians were often too frightened to complain or reclaim plundered goods. Soldiers could be fired up by the exhilaration of victory or the frustration of defeat. Successful sieges were often followed by more or less uncontrolled looting, whatever the terms of surrender. After the Royalists took Bristol in 1643 the soldiers turned to the countryside once they had finished with the city. Claiming that the country people were 'malignants', they held some to ransom and demanded protection money from others.[15] The prospect of plunder was one possible reason for volunteering for the armies; those who had been conscripted were often petty criminals, but, even if they were not, plunder offered some recompense for their enforced service and arrears of pay. The level of commitment of many soldiers, especially in the infantry, was questionable. Many changed sides after being taken prisoner and served well: both Fairfax and Cromwell said that some of their best soldiers were former cavaliers.[16] In 1647 Parliamentarian soldiers morris-danced through the streets of Worcester, calling the people roundhead dogs and roundhead whores.[17]

The armies' need for horses offered a convenient cover for horse-stealing (and those horses which were purchased might be severely undervalued). This happened even in the solidly Parliamentarian county of Hertfordshire: according to a complaint from East Barnet in December 1644 'divers pretending to be soldiers and other loose persons' demanded food and money 'in a bold and terrifying way'; the inhabitants complied 'for fear', but the exactions went on:

> during the time of quartering soldiers amongst us divers sheep, swine and poultry have been taken away by the soldiers, some in the presence of the owners . . . divers gates in the several grounds of the inhabitants as also their hedges and fences have been commonly broken, spoiled and carried away by the soldiers and . . . corn in the straw and some in the granary hath been taken and given to horses and spoiled.[18]

There was little question, in Hertfordshire, of Parliamentarian troops punishing a Royalist population, as was alleged at Compton House, but elsewhere plunder and quartering could be almost instruments of policy, designed to punish and subjugate a population or individuals seen as hostile, especially clergymen or Catholics; they were sometimes accompanied by wanton destruction.[19] Fired-up soldiers vandalized what they could not steal, encouraged (in the case of churches and cathedrals) by officers and preachers. Elsewhere they smashed and burned, slaughtered cattle and felled trees, with little concern for which side their owners were on. Some justified recourse to the sword by saying 'there was no other law now'.[20] And then there was the damage caused by the fighting itself. Sieges often caused immense physical destruction – the little Dorset town of Beaminster was almost destroyed, as was Taunton in the long Royalist siege in 1645. The damage wrought by the artillery and mines of the besiegers was often more than matched by the besieged; suburbs were flattened to deprive the attackers of cover and to open up the defenders' field of fire. At Exeter, where half the population lived in the suburbs, and which was held by each side in turn, all the buildings in two suburban parishes were demolished. By the end of the war between a third and a half of the inhabitants were homeless.[21] A successful siege was often followed by the sacking of the town, to reward the besieging soldiers and to punish the townspeople for their failure to surrender. Sieges and the suffering they caused, together with the fact that far more people were moving around the country than ever before – wives, camp followers and whores as well as soldiers – encouraged the spread of disease, not only plague but also smallpox and typhus. Because of the dispersed nature of the fighting, it is impossible to calculate accurately the numbers killed in the wars, but a plausible estimate is 80,000 killed in fighting and another 100,000 dying of disease and other causes related to the wars. This would give a percentage of the English population rather higher than that for the British dead in the First World War. The figures for Scotland were higher and for Ireland very much higher.[22]

The foregoing account has perhaps tended to emphasize the misdeeds of the Parliamentarian armies more than those of the Royalists, mainly because, as the victor, it was Parliament which had to contend with the pent-up force of civilian resentment at the end of the war. The king had tried, more than Parliament, to work with the traditional county authorities, to respect the rule of law and, where possible, to win consent. Many of his commanders, including Prince Rupert, had complied with his wishes in this, but it became increasingly hard to do so as the area under Royalist control shrank, first after Marston Moor, then after Naseby. There had always been some Royalists, especially those who had learned their soldiering on the Continent, who regarded the civilian author-ities as inherently uncooperative and believed that only the threat of force would make them truly compliant. Those trained abroad were also more liable to use violence against civilians. It was Rupert, after all, who ordered the sack of Leicester after the siege and the killing of civilians during the sack of Puritan Bolton: of between 1,200 and 1,500 killed, about 700 were civilians, at least half the town's peacetime population.[23] But these same professionals were also more likely to have learned the codes of conduct that prevailed on the Continent, especially in relation to giving quarter on the

battlefield and after sieges, and the treatment of prisoners.[24] If
the Royalists were responsible for some of the worst atrocities,
Parliamentarian officers were more than capable of brutality,
especially against Catholics and above all Irishmen. After the
siege of Basing House, which belonged to the Catholic
marquis of Winchester, about 100 of the garrison were killed,
300 were stripped (including women and the marquis) and the
house was set on fire.[25] (Although violence against women was
not uncommon, rape seems to have been very rare.)[26]
Parliament ordered in 1644 that all Irish Catholics taken on the
battlefield should be killed, in revenge for the Irish rising of
1641. The soldiers in the units that joined the king from Ireland
in 1643 were widely believed to be Irish Catholics, although
most were Protestants and many were English. After
Parliament captured Shrewsbury and Conway in 1645, Irish
prisoners were killed, as were Irish camp followers after
Naseby.[27] Rupert retaliated by killing English prisoners, telling
incredulous Parliamentarians that the Irish were just as much
the king's subjects as the English. The Irish apart, prisoners
were rarely killed, but they could be if a garrison had failed to
surrender by the time a breach had been made in the walls. On
the other hand, prisoners whose lives were spared were often
badly treated, being stripped and plundered, driven like cattle,
housed in bad conditions with little food. Small wonder that so
many changed sides.

Another reason for popular resentment of the Parliamentarian
war effort was its combination of ruthlessness, arbitrariness and
self-righteousness, seen partly in the treatment of Royalists and
partly in Parliament's programme of religious and moral reform.
Some of those identified as Royalists undoubtedly were just that:
those who had gone to join the king, or taken a commission in
his army, or sat in the Oxford Parliament, for example. But other
cases were more marginal. Sir John Boteler of Hertfordshire,
who served as a justice of the peace until the summer of 1643,
was accused of delinquency, before a committee of the House of
Commons. He admitted that he had received a commission of

array from the king, but claimed he had not acted on it. Indeed, he had sent it back 'because the country did not like it'. He was also accused of defending the commission, though one witness thought he had defended it but could not remember what he had said, and another could not remember his saying anything about it. Yet another said that Boteler was invited to a meeting about the commission, but did not come. Boteler admitted that he had disapproved of the raising of volunteers, believing that the trained bands were sufficient to defend the county, but denied that he had called the volunteers rogues; a witness said that he had 'seemed to second' others who had done so. Boteler admitted going to Oxford at the end of 1642 and bringing back a pardon from the king for the county if it ceased hostilities, but denied he had proclaimed it; the only witness could not say that he had. It also transpired that at a meeting at the house of one of Boteler's tenants, someone had alleged that he was a papist, at which he had become angry. He had also become angry when summoned to church to take the Covenant, especially as the minister there had been put in by Parliament; he feared that those who took the Covenant would suffer for it if the Royalists prevailed. He admitted keeping a chaplain, 'a learned, orthodox and sober man', described by his enemies as a priest. In response to claims that he had ignored the commands of Parliament, he produced proof that he had sent £200 to the Eastern Association headquarters at Cambridge; he later claimed he had contributed at least £1,200, plus a horse and arms to the value of £300. On the basis of these allegations and this evidence, the committee had imprisoned him for two years in London. He had soldiers on free quarter in his house, some of his tenants had given up their leases and others were in arrears.[28]

Boteler was doubtless one of many whose sympathies were Royalist, but who did not wish to risk all, or break with his neighbours, by actively supporting the king. He was undone by the allegations of people who styled themselves as godly and zealous for the cause, who were prepared to repeat rumour and hearsay, but hedged their own testimony with qualifications and vagueness. His cause was not helped by the fact that he became angry when traduced, or called a papist, by his social inferiors. It is most unlikely that the case against him would have stood up in a court of law, but parliamentary committees were not bound by the normal rules of procedure or evidence. At least Boteler had to contend only with Parliament. William Davenport of Bramhall, Cheshire, had his arms and horses confiscated by the Parliamentarians, was then plundered by the Royalists and eventually had his estates confiscated by Parliament.[29]

Even before the Covenant provided a touchstone of loyalty to Parliament's cause, the ordinance that established the Eastern Association had included an 'oath of association' to subscribe arms and money and defend the peace of the constituent counties. This was a weakened version of an oath which Pym had proposed earlier, modelled on the Covenant, 'not subject to equivocation', which was to be tendered to show 'who are for us and who are against us'.[30] In 1644 Sir William Waller denounced neutrals, who 'neither regard the miserable condition of our brethren in other counties, the present danger of their own, nor the cause of God'. As they did nothing for the common cause, or the glory of God 'we shall take them for no other than enemies of the state' and proceed against them accordingly.[31] Men who held such views had no time for the ties of kinship and neighbourliness, or the visceral fear of bloodshed, which had underlain the neutrality schemes of 1642. But for many, respect for kin and neighbours was an essential feature of a civilized society and they responded to the divisions and bloodshed of civil war with calls for reconciliation. In fact, some leading Parliamentarians were prepared to help their Royalist friends and kin. The commander of the Eastern Association army, the earl of Manchester, helped mitigate the effects of the sequestration of the estates of the Royalist, Lord Capel, and in the 1650s Cromwell's second in command, John Lambert, helped his Catholic relatives to recover their lands. In some counties moderates gained control over sequestration and allowed Royalists to recover their lands in return for modest payments, provoking angry complaints from hardliners. Even so, for many, the 'fiery spirits' in Parliament were leading England into a dark unknown world of violence and hatred.

Those sequestered and imprisoned for Royalism were defenceless against their enemies, who ruthlessly took advantage of their situation. Household goods were sold off at knock-down prices, along with any moveable assets on their estates, especially timber. Manchester had secured Parliament's agreement that Lord Capel's Parliamentarian brother should manage his estates, but these were scattered over several counties and, during one of the brother's absences, the committee at Hertford ordered that over a thousand trees should be felled and the timber sold to raise money for the war effort. Tenants withheld rents and local people helped themselves to goods, stock and materials, confident that they could do so with impunity. In times of dislocation and confusion, the unscrupulous found it easy to prey on the vulnerable; the parishioners of East Barnet suspected that some of those demanding money and food were not genuine soldiers, but they did not think it politic to argue. When soldiers fled after a battle, or marched away without their weapons after surrendering, they were often plundered and stripped by soldiers from the other side, but also by civilians: Essex's soldiers sufferer grievously at the hands of Cornish men and women after Lostwithiel.[32] Civilians as well as soldiers plundered corpses on the battlefield and finished off the dying.

The yields from the sequestered estates were disappointing. At a time when even Parliamentarian landlords were finding it hard to secure more than a fraction of the rents due from their tenants, and many farmers were abandoning their tenancies, it was difficult to lease farms out for more than modest rents, but county committees tended to be hostile to proposals that sequestered landlords should be allowed to regain their lands for a lump sum. They complained bitterly when military commanders granted surrender articles which protected Royalists from sequestration. The commanders, however, insisted that, having granted the articles, they were honour bound to uphold them. It is likely that some of those who managed sequestered estates were incompetent and inexperienced, but there were inevitably accusations of corruption. Members of county committees and their officials were paid attendance fees or salaries and were able to claim expenses for subsistence while on committee business. Some possibly bought timber or goods from sequestered estates at very low prices. Certainly some later purchased crown and church lands, or those sold off by heavily indebted Royalists; as the land market was glutted and there was a fear that the lands might be repossessed in the future, they were able to purchase them cheaply. More generally, the complexity of the collection and spending of money, and of the process of sequestration, together with the vast sums handled, meant that suspicions of embezzlement were found among moderate Parliamentarians as well as Royalists. Hence the creation of accounts committees, the main purpose of which was to seek evidence of the misappropriation of public money.

The bloodshed, destruction and economic disruption inevitably created a sense of dislocation and disorientation. This was compounded by a sustained attack on the settled habits of religious life. The Book of Common Prayer set out a cycle of observances for the Christian year: not just the major festivals of Christmas, Easter and the like, but also prayers at seedtime and thanksgiving at harvest. It was customary in many places to walk or beat the bounds of the parish at Rogationtide, an expression of communal identity and unity, often followed by a dinner. The major rites of passage of parishioners took place within the church and for each – baptism, marriage and burial – the Prayer Book provided a familiar rubric. Where this had not been prohibited by Puritan authorities, the church also provided a venue for collective sociability, such as church ales or wakes. The essence of Common Prayer was that it was indeed 'common' – inclusive rather than exclusive. Communion was open to all adults who were not out of charity with their neighbours, which in itself provided an incentive to reconciliation. But the Puritans who dominated Parliament and the county committees, had no such inclusive vision. They divided society firmly into the godly few and the ungodly many. They also eagerly seized the opportunity to root the last dregs of Rome out of parish worship and to purge the parishes of 'scandalous' ministers. At first, the work of purification had won considerable support. Railing off the altar at the east end of the church had proved contentious in many parishes, as had Laud's promotion of the 'beauty of holiness' in general. But it soon became apparent that the 'fiery spirits' in Parliament wished to go much further than simply reversing Laud's innovations. In August 1643 a Parliamentary ordinance ordered the destruction of crucifixes, candles and images of saints (but not of the devil or Old Testament figures). In East Anglia William Dowsing destroyed hundreds of 'superstitious' pictures and even defaced gravestones bearing the legend 'pray for our souls'. Godly magistrates tried, not always successfully, to pull down market crosses. Charing Cross, in London, suffered this fate. In 1644 organs, fonts and the wearing of surplices were banned. At the end of the year Parliament forbade the celebration of Christmas, probably at the behest of the Scots: there was a marked hostility towards Christmas in Scotland until the latter part of the twentieth century. This prohibition was later extended to all other festivals of the traditional Christian calendar.

The programme followed by Parliament was overwhelmingly negative and destructive. It was driven by a visceral hatred for anything that savoured of popery, but also a moral revulsion against excess, self-indulgence and the pleasures of the senses. Morris-dancing and the erection of maypoles were condemned because they encouraged drunkenness and promiscuity. Christmas was associated with a great deal of eating and drinking, with music and dancing and often a strong element of licensed misrule: conduct (or misconduct) was tolerated at such times which would not normally be acceptable. But Christmas was also a time to be celebrated with family, friends and neighbours: eating and drinking together strengthened social ties. Above all it was fun – not a word that featured in the vocabulary of Puritans. The prohibition of familiar rubrics and rituals, which for many brought spiritual edification, left people bereft and angry. Keeping the second Sunday of every month as a day of thanksgiving was hardly a substitute for Easter or Christmas. Even the satisfaction of celebrating communion with neighbours at Easter was denied to many parishes; Parliament's official policy was to confine access to communion to those certified by the minister to be truly godly. The requirement that those receiving had to be in charity with their neighbours no longer applied; those outside the inner ring of the godly were now excluded. It is significant that, whereas Parliament's order in 1641 to remove altars and altar rails was often obeyed with alacrity, the commissioners who came to destroy images and 'purify' church interiors met with significant opposition and obstruction.

The process of destruction was replicated in the Church of England's government and administration. Church courts had been effectively stripped of their powers by the Act abolishing High Commission in 1641. Episcopacy was not formally abolished until 1646, although both Houses had agreed to its abolition early in 1643. Parliament was also slow to move towards the banning of Common Prayer, partly because the matter was being discussed in the Westminster Assembly of Divines. However, from 1641 some Puritan ministers ceased to use the Prayer Book and the Commons refused to reprimand them. There was sufficient alarm among traditional Prayer Book Anglicans about the way things were going for numerous petitions to be presented to Parliament, defending its use, in the first half of 1642. Not until January 1645 was the use of the Prayer Book forbidden; instead, parishes were ordered to use the Directory, drawn up by the Westminster Assembly. Unlike Common Prayer, the Directory contained no set forms for services, but provided a basic statement of (Calvinist) Christian beliefs, leaving it to ministers to construct and conduct services as they saw fit. As the Westminster Assembly and Parliament, between them, failed to establish an effective new form of church government to replace epis-copacy, ministers – and parishes – were left in large part to their own devices. The absence of a machinery of supervision and coercion meant that it was difficult for Parliament or the county committees to monitor what was happening in the parishes and especially to prevent the use of the Prayer Book. There is no known instance of a minister being punished for using Common Prayer, but numerous cases (throughout the late 1640s and the 1650s) of ministers being presented for *failing* to use it. There were claims that the Act of Uniformity of 1559, which required use of the Prayer Book, was still in force. Some ministers were forced to use the Prayer Book by threats of violence and those who disrupted Prayer Book services were driven out with blows and jeers. Parishioners forcibly resisted the intrusion of new godly ministers.[33]

The parish remained the basic unit of religious worship. Until 1650 everyone was required by law to attend their parish church on pain of a fine, although this ceased to be enforced in the 1640s. People were also required to pay tithes, to provide maintenance for the parish minister and in some cases the stipend of ministers was increased in the later 1640s, as tithes hitherto collected by Royalist laymen were returned to the parish. In the absence of effective church government, the key figure in determining the nature of parish worship was the minister. Apart from legislation forbidding traditional prac-tices, the main weapon of Parliament and the county committees, in their drive to bring reformation to the parishes, was the removal of 'scandalous' ministers. In deciding who was 'scandalous', they relied on denunciations by the local godly. The most common accusations were of 'drunkenness' and insufficient preaching – both thoroughly subjective charges – or lack of commitment to the Parliamentary cause. There was the usual mixture of hearsay, innuendo and unsubstantiated allegations: ministers were often accused of 'having spoken against Parliament', or having refused to contribute to the Parliamentary war effort.[34] Sometimes, when ministers were removed, their parishioners rejoiced, but often their removal was resisted. Their replacements were denied access to the parsonage or the church, or received no tithes; in some cases the previous incumbent was reinstated by force. Some parishes lobbied so vigorously against the removal of a popular minister that the county committee decided not to insist on ejecting him.

As for the nature of parish worship, the evidence is sparse. There was no comprehensive machinery for gathering information from the parishes, and those which continued to use the Prayer Book and the old rituals were not likely to advertise the fact. It is clear that the great majority of young clergymen ordained in the 1640s were ordained by bishops, even after the abolition of episcopacy. Parliament made no provision for ordination without bishops until 1646, and even then the new system was slow to get going. There is clear evidence that parishes received communion at Christmas, Easter and other forbidden festival days, and hints that this was open communion, rather than the closed communion, confined to the godly, favoured by Parliament. Overall, it seems clear that attempts to kill off the old Prayer Book services, engrained in people's minds and hearts over several generations, failed. They bounced back, along with morris-dancing and maypoles, at the Restoration; in many parishes the Prayer Book was being used well before it was again required by law in 1662.

Resistance to the intrusion of unwanted ministers was considerably less dangerous than attempting to resist the depredations of soldiers, but the Clubmen movement, which reached its peak in 1645–6, attempted to do just that. There had been an earlier, and different, use of the term 'Clubmen' in 1642–3. The resistance of clothworkers to Royalist plundering in the West Riding of Yorkshire grew into a mass insurgency, led by Sir Thomas Fairfax, the future commander of the New

Model. His fellow commanders, gentlemen to a man, were appalled by the dangers involved in encouraging popular violence: several defected to the king.[35] In 1645 many thousands appeared in arms in a variety of southern and Midland counties, complaining of the depredations of soldiers and tax-collectors from both sides: their aim was 'to keep off both Parliament's forces and the king's also from contribution and quarter in their county'.[36] Some complained that 'the true worship of Almighty God and our religion are almost forgotten'.[37] There can be no question that this was a genuinely popular movement, invoking against both sides the right of resistance which Parliament had claimed against the king. In places, the local gentry, clergy and lawyers attempted to channel the movement, particularly on behalf of the king, but the farmers and craftsmen who formed the backbone of the movement made it clear that their quarrel was with the misdeeds of soldiers on both sides. In some areas the Royalists sought to harness popular resentment of Parliament's taxation.

In the Welsh Marches in the winter of 1644–5 the king encouraged the formation of an 'association'. The king granted its request to raise soldiers and levy local taxes and receive the profits of the sequestration of Parliamentarians. He was less willing to grant its request to choose its own officers, or to enforce the orders of the Oxford Parliament about military discipline. The local Royalist commanders were even less impressed, and saw the association as undermining their capacity to organize the army. For many of the peasantry, the association seemed an irrelevance: they wanted fewer soldiers and taxes, not more. Matters came to a head in Herefordshire. The governor of Hereford demanded contributions, the local people refused to pay, and the soldiers killed several. There followed a mass rising, which called for the removal of all Royalist troops from the county. The rising was put down by Rupert and his brother Maurice. The insurgents were punished and, in effect, military rule established over the county.[38] Elsewhere, armed resistance to the military was more successful, especially where the terrain favoured guerilla warfare. Around Gloucester, where high hedges made it impossible to use cavalry, country people picked off stragglers and took revenge for plunder. The Royalist governor of Berkeley Castle could not send soldiers out to collect victuals, because the people would kill them; they also harassed scouts and messengers. There was similar popular action against the Royalists in Somerset and against Essex's army in Cornwall.[39]

The events in the Marches showed that Royalist loyalty had its limits even in the Royalist heartlands. The same was true in South Wales, where in the summer of 1645 Charles authorized the raising of the entire male population. In Glamorgan 4,000 men were drawn up. Their leaders requested the right to elect their own officers, which was granted. They took the name 'Peaceable Army' and demanded that they be led by local gentlemen, not outsiders, and that the tax burden be reduced to a bearable level. The 'Army' forced the governor of Cardiff to hand over the town. By now the fortunes of the king were obviously on the wane. When news came that Parliament had taken Bristol, the 'Peaceable Army' declared for Parliament.[40] What had been intended as an attempt to mobilize additional men and money for the king had ended up achieving just the opposite. In the absence of regular troops to coerce them, and with the king's hopes fading fast, the men of Glamorgan pursued what they saw as their own best interests.

If the most immediate concern of the Clubmen was to get rid of the soldiers and reduce the burden of taxation, they also claimed that both king and Parliament had lost sight of the original objectives of the war: to secure the rights of subjects and the rule of law. These objectives could be achieved only through a national settlement, in which the Clubmen were far more willing than Parliament to see the king offered generous terms. Many were as hostile to county committees as they were to soldiers, and called for the restoration of the old forms of local government – 'known ways', including (for many) Elizabethan and Jacobean forms of worship – and county government put back in the hands of the old ruling families.[41] Both sides hoped to recruit the Clubmen to their cause, but they had their own agenda: if they seemed more hostile to one side than the other, that was generally because one side was predominant in their area and its soldiers posed the greater threat to them. If some seemed to prefer to deal with Fairfax and the New Model, that was because his men were better disciplined (and better paid) than some of the wild and brutal Royalists. But if their local demands were designed to protect them from both sides, their proposals for a national settlement were more acceptable to the Royalists than to Parliament. Moreover, the final collapse of the king's cause meant the surrender and disbanding of the Royalist armies. Now all the burden on civilians, and all the maltreatment, came from the Parliamentarian armies. The accumulated resentment of four years of bloody war was focused on Parliament. Above all there was the insistent demand that Parliament should take the first crucial step towards a return to normal by negotiating a settlement with the king.

7

THE RISE OF THE ARMY

Any hopes that the king's surrender would be followed by a return to normality and order were quickly dashed. The military presence remained enormous, even after the Royalists had dispersed. The Scots did not go home until February1647, and only a part of Parliament's forces had been disbanded by the spring of that year. The civilian population had to lodge and feed many thousands of soldiers; as they had to be paid – and indeed their pay fell further into arrears – taxation remained at the wartime level. Free quarter continued, and if anything became worse because of the soldiers' lack of pay. The bad habits of wartime – the requisitioning that shaded into plunder, the casual theft, the arrogant violence – continued too. The disgruntled Scots and the disbanded Royalists making their way home behaved just as badly. Many county committees continued to act arbitrarily and brutally towards those they regarded as 'malignants' or trouble-makers, and towards the accounts committees who were trying to investigate their management of public moneys. Complaints of over-assessment, and over-collection, of taxation continued. Meanwhile, civilian complaints and resistance increased. These complaints were now more likely to find a sympathetic hearing since in some counties the regular machinery of local government began to be restored, despite the resistance of the county committees; some county bosses, notably in Kent and Somerset, managed to pack the commission of the peace with their supporters. But in Lincolnshire the chairman of the quarter sessions, himself a Parliamentarian colonel, urged people not to pay the excise and the grand jury presented it as a grievance. Resistance to the excise, and violence against those trying to collect it, became more common. In Norwich, in December 1646, a butcher was arrested for refusing to pay the meat excise. A crowd of angry butchers gathered, those who tried to escort the butcher out of the city were badly beaten up, and the local excise officers went in fear their lives. Small wonder that excise officers began to use soldiers to help collect the tax – which further added to its unpopularity. There was similar resistance to the excise in London, from both brewers and butchers, which culminated in the Smithfield riots, in which the excise office was burned down. This was followed by the withdrawal of the excise duty on meat and salt – though the duty on strong beer was doubled. There was also widespread refusal in London to pay the assessment which provided the pay for the hated New Model Army.[1]

With the ending of hostilities in the summer of 1646 there was a general expectation that there would be a settlement with the king; but by whom and on what terms? After the king's defeat there was a surge of feeling in his favour. Not only did he no longer constitute a threat, but his sufferings earned him sympathy. The aura of divinity which had always surrounded the monarchy (and which he had sought to cultivate) now revived in his depiction as a Christ-like figure. Many flocked to be touched for the 'king's evil'.[2] Some Royalists argued that the experience of 'parliamentary tyranny' showed that a full restoration of the king's powers was a lesser evil than crippling taxes, rapacious officials and predatory soldiers. Most of the demands of the Clubmen did not go that far, although they were often somewhat vague, but they seemed to suggest that a settlement on the basis of the reforms of 1641 would be acceptable; certainly the dismantling of the current fiscal and military regime was an urgent necessity. But Parliament had gone to war because it was convinced that the 1641 reforms offered an insufficient guarantee against renewed royal misrule. Others had a very different understanding of 'parliamentary tyranny'. Some of Parliament's more radical supporters had been led by Parliament's declarations to expect greater freedom for the people and more respect for their property, but instead they were faced with an authoritarian regime, which imposed unprecedented levels of taxation and dealt brutally with critics and dissidents. John Lilburne, imprisoned by Star Chamber in the 1630s, was imprisoned at different times by each of the Houses in the 1640s. It seemed that members had been corrupted by power, so that, while it was necessary to curb the power of the king, it was also necessary to curb the power of Parliament. This could be done partly by making MPs genuinely accountable to those they represented, through frequent elections and a more equitable electoral system, and partly by limiting their competence. Those who became known as the Levellers took the concept of the 'fundamental laws', much used by Parliament in its declarations, and turned it from a rather nebulous term for the general principles underlying the ancient constitution into a precise written statement of what Parliament could and could not do. This statement – a written constitution – was to derive its authority over Parliament from popular endorsement. It was to be, literally, an agreement of the people.

For the moment neither the proposals of the Clubmen nor those of the Levellers stood any chance of winning acceptance at Westminster. The major groups in Parliament were in agreement on some points. The king would have to share with Parliament his power to choose his advisers and his power to command the armed forces, although it was not entirely clear whether this was to be for a period of years or permanently. Some Royalists should be punished for what would now be called war crimes; more generally Royalists should be debarred from holding offices or voting in Parliamentary elections for a period of years. The king would also have to agree to the abolition of bishops. Despite the studied ambiguity of the Solemn League and Covenant, leaving room to argue that the English had not promised to introduce full-blown Scottish Presbyterianism, there was no way the terms of the League could be used to sanction the retention of episcopacy. So the bishops were abolished, the very least the English Parliament could do for the Scots under the circumstances, and many were happy to do it. The imposition of the Directory and the banning of the celebration of Christmas, both at the behest of the Scots, added to Parliament's unpopularity.

Of all the issues that divided Parliament, religion was the most contentious. Even before the war broke out, there had been growing anxiety about damage to the fabric of parish churches, departures from the Prayer Book services, and the proliferation of gathered churches. One reason for this seeming disintegration was that the power of the bishops had effectively collapsed; it became totally ineffectual amid the chaos of civil war. The dramatic breakdown of episcopacy gave a substantial boost to millenarian expectations of radical change on earth. Millenarian beliefs were based on the more prophetic books of the Bible, especially Daniel and Revelation. They had always been an important part of Protestant thought. John Foxe's *Acts and Monuments*, or book of martyrs, probably the most widely read book after the Bible, used an interpretation of these books as the basis of its chronology. Revelation is, to put it mildly, a difficult book, full of strange beasts and numbers. It could be interpreted in various ways, but it was clear that it described the final phase of history, in which a cataclysmic struggle between the forces of Christ and of Antichrist ended with the defeat of the latter and the thousand-year rule of the saints. The book is full of images of overturning, as the great and wealthy of the world are cast down and the humble, the meek and the persecuted are raised up. It inspired a variety of popular revolts in the late Middle Ages, and for some in the 1640s it offered a blueprint for revolutionary action. A belief in God's all-pervading providence could lead those who were consistently successful to believe that they were God's chosen instruments; the saints should seize power and establish the rule of the godly over the ungodly. Others were less certain, preferring to watch God's will unfolding through events, and relying on God to overturn the old order in His own good time. Many believed that they were living through the great struggle, prophesied in Revelation, between Antichrist (normally identified with the papacy) and Christ: the Thirty Years' War on the Continent, generally seen in England as a religious war, seemed to fit the description exactly.

Millenarianism, like anti-popery, became a major element of the Parliamentarian mindset. It gave those who held it a conviction that they were acting out God's plan for the history of the world. The saints looked forward eagerly to Christ's second coming and the day of judgement, after which they would find everlasting rest, a welcome change after the travails of earthly life. For the godly, worldly things were a distraction from the serious business of seeking out God's purposes and preparing for the afterlife. 'Freedom' for such people meant freedom to submit themselves to the will of God; those who joined gathered churches signed up to their codes of discipline. These gathered churches, as they renounced the authority of the national church, might look anarchic and subversive to outside observers, but their members practised a rigorous self-discipline; they did not need to be forced to behave by an outside authority. On the other hand, their confidence that they would be saved, and that they were in the right, gave them a moral certainty in whatever they undertook, which made them formidable soldiers and stubborn adversaries. While they were eager to win converts, they were demanding about who they would admit: only 'visible saints' who would accept the rules of membership. Their view of a church as a voluntary association of true believers was very different from that of the established church, which comprised the whole community and so inevitably mixed saints and sinners. The gathered churches, conscious of the imminence of the second coming, separated themselves from the national church and distanced themselves from the ungodly. Utterly convinced of their rightness, they were intolerant of the views of others and engaged in acrimonious debates with one another and with the parish clergy, but they believed in the power of argument rather than coercion. They argued that religion was a matter for the individual conscience and that the secular authorities had no right to meddle with it.

It should be stressed that the gathered churches comprised only a small minority of the population and indeed a minority of those who saw themselves as godly. The majority of Puritan ministers and laypeople accepted the need for a national church, based on the traditional parish system and funded by tithes, which many of the gathered churches denounced as an unfair exaction. (Some gathered churches, however, were formed by ministers holding parishes in the national church, effectively 'unchurching' those parishioners who did not want to join.) For most Puritans, the argument, from Elizabeth's reign to Charles I's, had been about what sort of national church there should be. Puritans wanted to purify the services of 'popish' ceremonies, and were outraged when the Laudians added new ones. They wanted freedom for the clergy to preach, to edify and inspire the laity, and were appalled when Laud and Charles I restricted the amount of preaching and the topics on which they could preach. They also harboured an ideal of effective parish-based moral discipline, of the sort that had developed in the Calvinist churches on the Continent, and in Scotland. Painfully aware of the natural sinfulness of humankind, they believed that their parishioners should be saved from themselves by wholesome admonition to mend their ways and, if they failed to do so, by exemplary punishment; this often involved standing before the congregation in a white sheet, with a paper stating the nature of their offence (drunkenness, fornication or whatever). Puritan ministers naturally assumed that they should play a key part in this process, as their counterparts did in Scotland, but in England the main instruments of moral discipline were the church courts which (according to the Puritans) were more interested in punishing the principled nonconformity of the godly clergy than the moral lapses of the laity. Although they taught that good works could play no part in salvation, they also believed that the whole community could be punished by God for the sins of some of its members. When lightning struck the spire of the parish church of Dorchester in 1613, starting a devastating fire, its doughty pastor took this as a signal to begin a campaign of moral purification in the town.

The collapse of episcopal authority from 1640 seemed to offer the Puritans their chance. Some, with the blessing of the House of Commons, ceased to use the Prayer Book. In 1642 Parliament set up, at Westminster, an assembly of divines, as demanded by the Grand Remonstrance, to consider the future shape of the Church of England. The debates of the Westminster Assembly soon became linked to Parliament's negotiations with the Scots, and after the Solemn League and Covenant a number of Scottish ministers were added to the Assembly. Although the majority clearly favoured some sort of Presbyterianism, they were stubbornly opposed by ministers from gathered churches, who called for toleration, at least for the godly. There were also lay members of the Assembly, and many in Parliament, who thought that Scottish Presbyterianism gave the clergy too much power over the laity and that it was necessary for the state to retain control over matters of religion, which were too important to be left to the clergy. MPs resented still more the claims of some clergy that Presbyterian church government was ordained by God and that Parliament had no right to meddle wit it. On the other hand, many Puritan ministers were outraged at the growth of the gathered churches, whom they accused of appalling heresies and moral degradation; the Baptists practised adult baptism, and the press revelled in stories of lecherous pastors baptizing nubile virgins. The gathered churches were also denounced for undermining the concept of a national church, embracing the entire community. One of their most outspoken critics, Thomas Edwards, produced a lengthy work, *Gangraena*, which depicted them as a cancer, eating away at the body of the Church.

The gathered churches also had their friends. Their adherents were strong in the army; many regiments became hotbeds of religious discussion and piety. Baxter claimed that 'hot headed sectaries' in the army denounced the king as a tyrant who could not be trusted.[3] In Parliament followers of the Saye–St John group, who became known as Independents, supported a degree of freedom for the godly, not least to maintain the goodwill and sustain the effectiveness of the army. In addition, by 1645 the Independents no longer saw any need to pander to the Scots: indeed, they regarded them with open hostility. While not opposed to the provision of better preaching and godly worship in the parishes, they saw this as being quite compatible with toleration for those of the godly who chose to separate from the national church. Their opponents, led by Holles, became known as Presbyterians. Urged on by the English Presbyterian clergy, they were deeply concerned by the spread of heresy and the restless questioning of authority in matters of religion. Unfettered debate led not to truth but to confusion and despair, and it was necessary to lay down the basics of orthodox doctrine and to compel preachers to subscribe to them. The problem was to secure agreement as to what those basics were, but also many laymen did not like being told by clergymen what to believe. Some of the gathered churches, especially the Baptists, questioned the authority of ministers to explain Scripture. The ministers argued that their training at the universities, in Greek and Hebrew, gave them access to the originals of Scriptural texts, but the Baptists argued that the ability to understand the Bible came directly from divine inspiration, while educated laymen claimed that they were as well able to understand the original texts as any minister. Nevertheless, the Presbyterians in Parliament, and the Presbyterian clergy outside, believed that the lid had to be put back on the Pandora's box that had been opened since 1640. They also had some sympathy for the religious aspirations of the Scots, and were appalled by the Independents' unilateral abandonment of the Solemn League and Covenant.

Amid these contending forces the debates of the Westminster Assembly ground on. The Presbyterians argued that some form of government had to be provided for the Church in place of episcopacy. The Independents were not against this, so long as it had no power to coerce the gathered churches. What eventually emerged was a half-baked Presbyterian system. Each parish was to have elders to assist the pastor, as in Scotland; but any organization above the parish level was to be voluntary, so that the pastor and elders would have no coercive powers and submission to discipline by parishioners would be voluntary, as in the gathered churches. There could be no appeal to the secular authorities, as in Scotland, to make discipline work, and no use of secular penalties, such as excommunication. In some areas a rudimentary organization above the parish level was established, notably in London and Lancashire, and there was cooperation between the clergy, for example in checking the qualifications and fitness of those aspiring to the ministry. But overall the dreams of the Puritan clergy of an effective system of parish-based discipline had been dashed by the Independents and by the anti-clericalism of many MPs.

It is difficult to tell what was happening in the parishes where the great majority of English people worshipped. From the 1630s to the 1660s, most of the clergy seem to have adapted to changing official forms of worship with surprising ease. Where

Royalists owned the right to collect the tithes, or to nominate the minister, these were confiscated along with their lands; the tithes were used to provide a proper maintenance and the right of nomination was used to install a godly minister. Some godly ministers, like Richard Baxter at Kidderminster, practised an inclusive ministry, adapting their demands to fit the differing capabilities of their flocks. Others, frustrated of their hopes of gaining effective coercive powers over the ungodly, concentrated their attentions on those they saw as godly and ignored the rest. What does seem clear is that there was widespread resentment of the changes in the parishes, yet again underlining the deep roots that Common Prayer had put down in the people's spiritual consciousness by 1640.

Parliament's total lack of accord on religion would not necessarily prove a serious handicap when it came to reaching a settlement with Charles I. On one point, though, there was wide agreement – the abolition of bishops. Charles, of course, was unlikely to agree to this willingly, but in the summer of 1646 it seemed to most in Parliament that he was in no position to quibble. He had been resoundingly defeated in the civil war and those who were defeated in war always had to make concessions. Charles, however, did not see it that way. This had been neither a normal nor a just war, but an unnatural rebellion. The 'rebels' had been in the wrong, the king had been in the right, and his defeat did not change that in any way. Charles simply did not see why he should make concessions. He was being asked to sign away some of the most basic powers of the monarchy, which in his view were not his to hand over: they belonged to the monarchy, not to him, and he would have to answer to God for his stewardship as king. It might be acceptable for him to cede these powers for a period of years, possibly even for his lifetime, but he could not bind his successors, or pass on to them an emasculated monarchy. Similarly, he believed that he could not abandon episcopacy; he also regarded Presbyterianism as incompatible with monarchy. 'The nature of Presbyterian government', he wrote, 'is to steal or force the crown from the king's head; for their chief maxim is . . . that all kings must submit to Christ's kingdom, of which they are the sole governors.'[4] His Catholic queen, for whom all forms of Protestantism were equally false, urged him to abandon episcopacy temporarily; this would win over the Presbyterians, and he could always re-establish it once he had regained effective power. Charles replied that his conscience would not allow him to do this. Given his track record of deceit and duplicity, it may seem incongruous that Charles should be so swayed by his conscience, but on this occasion he was probably sincere (we know this not least because his protestations of conscience are in his private correspondence with his wife). Faced with Parliament's arguments in terms of negotiation and expediency, Charles replied that certain matters were simply non-negotiable. Even arguments for the primacy of religion, however, included an element of calculation: 'people are governed by pulpits more than the word in times of peace'. Control of the church was more important than control over the militia. 'Religion is the only firm foundation of all power; [if] that [is] cast loose or depraved no government can be stable; for when was there ever obedience where religion did not teach it?'[5]

However sincere Charles may have been, there were inevitably elements of calculation mixed in with his commitment to principle. He was well aware of the divisions among his opponents, which is why he surrendered to the Scots, rather than to the New Model or the English Parliament. He was also aware of the growing calls around the nation for his more or less unconditional restoration to power. These calls grew louder when, in the absence of a settlement, the armies were kept in being. Wartime levels of taxation continued, as did free quarter, plundering and indiscipline. The longer this continued, the greater would be the pressure on Parliament to reach agreement with the king on almost any terms. Charles assumed that any settlement, to be viable, would have to be based on monarchy and this, with the divisions among his opponents, gave him a very strong bargaining position, despite his defeat. 'You cannot be without me,' he told army leaders in 1647, 'you will fall to ruin if I do not sustain you.'[6] During the war, the Presbyterians had always seemed the more inclined to reach a settlement with him, but, even without pressure from the Scots, they were implacably opposed to the restoration of episcopacy. The Independents were more flexible on this point: provided the gathered churches enjoyed their freedom, they were less concerned about the form of the established church. For them, a non-coercive episcopacy was as acceptable as an ineffectual Presbyterianism – and more acceptable than a coercive Presbyterianism. In the aftermath of Parliament's victory, in the negotiations with the king the alignments that had prevailed for much of the civil war shifted and became blurred. Strange alliances were formed, and men behaved in ways that others found difficult to explain. Events moved with bewildering rapidity, and contemporaries, unlike historians, did not have the benefit of hindsight to aid in making sense of them. But hindsight can also be dangerous: one should not transpose back in time attitudes and aspirations that developed later.

After the war ended, the Presbyterians, led by Holles, began to gain the ascendancy in the Commons. Although contemporaries talked of 'parties', and discussed their workings with great interest, it seems that only a minority of the Commons could be described as behaving with any sort of consistency. In between there was a large body of uncommitted MPs, who inclined to one side or the other depending on circumstances. During 1645 and the first half of 1646 the Independents were dominant. Their aggressive approach to winning the war seemed to offer the best hope of ending hostilities, and their outspoken denunciations of the Scots echoed the dislike and disillusionment felt by many, especially in the North. But with the war over, the Presbyterians seemed to offer the best prospect of returning to peacetime normality; the Independents were too closely associated with the New Model. In addition, the Presbyterians' firm hostility towards the gathered churches and incipient religious anarchy was widely shared. There may also have been a perception that the Presbyterians were the more likely to reach a settlement with the king; if so, it was mistaken. Nevertheless, the latter part of 1646 was a time of Presbyterian resurgence, not only in Parliament but also in London. The Independents, concerned that the City's rulers seemed lukewarm towards the war effort, had deprived them of control over the trained bands. This clearly rankled among the citizens, among whom Presbyterianism was extremely strong; there was also a high concentration of heavyweight Presbyterian preachers in the City. In December 1646 the Presbyterians won a sweeping victory in the common council elections, and there were growing calls to restore the City's control over its own affairs in general and the trained bands in particular. A petition to Parliament called for the disbandment of the New Model as a nest of heretics.[7]

As London was the only source of loans and paid a major share of the excise, it exercised a disproportionately large influence over the government. Its financial clout was especially significant at a time when the Presbyterians in Parliament were beginning to disband the armies. Over the winter of 1646–7 the Presbyterians strengthened their hold on the Commons, especially after persuading the Scots forces to go home, which removed the possibility that the king might negotiate an unsatisfactory deal with them. The king was handed over to parliamentary commissioners on 30 January. He was treated with studied discourtesy: he was not allowed his chaplains or household servants and it was ordered that he was not to be shown the respect normally accorded to kings until he had accepted Parliament's terms.[8] The Presbyterians also gained a stranglehold on the Derby House Committee: initially responsible for the reduction of Ireland, this increasingly became the key policy-making committee, with particular reference to the army. By the spring the Western army and part of the Northern army had been disbanded, without receiving their full arrears; the unspoken assumption of many in Parliament was that the soldiers did not deserve to receive all their arrears, because they had stolen so much from civilians. Parliament then turned its attention to the New Model, which comprised about one-half of the forces still on foot. As Parliament had announced that it was (at last) going to send an army to reconquer Ireland, it seemed strange that the Derby House Committee should be choosing to disband the most effective force at its disposal, instead of sending it to Ireland. It would seem that it was moved more by political than by military considerations. The New Model was seen as a hotbed of religious radicalism, and had ignored Parliamentary ordinances forbidding lay preaching. Many officers had not subscribed the Covenant and the third part of *Gangraena*, published in December 1646, focused on the army. It had also been one of the major supports of the Parliamentary Independents, who had considered using it against the Scots. On the other hand, it had made less use of 'industrial action' – holding county committeemen or mayors to ransom in order to secure pay – than other armies, perhaps because it had less need to, as it was paid more regularly. It may also have been seen as radical in politics. It contained many of the most zealous and committed officers and soldiers among the Parliamentarian forces, and these almost certainly discussed the cause they were fighting for and the sort of new order they hoped to see after the war. But there is very little evidence of independent political action on the part of the New Model. It showed due respect to Parliament, which had brought it into being, and addressed it by means of petitions. Until March 1647 Parliament had responded to some of the demands in these petitions, and the soldiers had no reason to suspect that it would not go on doing so.[9]

During March the Derby House Committee made it clear which units they intended to send to Ireland, which they planned to use as a small standing army at home, and which were to be disbanded. All officers would be required to conform to the Presbyterian Church, which the Committee hoped would soon be established. Resentment grew within the army at the speed with which the process was being rushed through, and the lack of provision for the legitimate concerns of the soldiers. At times, it seemed, the Presbyterians could barely hide their contempt and loathing for the New Model. After much discussion, at meetings and in the press, the Commons heard that a petition was circulating in the army. It was to be presented, not to Parliament, but to the commander-in-chief, Sir Thomas Fairfax. He was peremptorily ordered to suppress it, but it continued to circulate. On 29 March several Presbyterian MPs, who were members of the army, claimed that the petition was being promoted by senior officers. On the basis of these unsubstantiated and, for the most part, fictitious allegations, the Commons again ordered the suppression of the petition and later, in a thin House, passed a 'Declaration of Dislike'. This accused the army of conduct akin to mutiny, attempting to place conditions on Parliament and obstructing the relief of Ireland. It declared that all who continued to promote the petition 'shall be looked upon as enemies of the state and disturbers of the public peace'.[10]

It should be emphasized that this petition had not yet been presented, to Fairfax or to anyone else, and could reasonably be seen as an internal army document. Its contents and tone were hardly confrontational. It stressed the army's faithful service to Parliament and made some specific requests, starting with an indemnity from prosecution for actions in time or place of war; already civilians were prosecuting soldiers for such actions, and they feared magistrates and juries would be biased against them. The soldiers distinguished between actions as soldiers in the service of Parliament, and actions while soldiers, in an unofficial capacity, and claimed that they should be exempt from prosecution for the former. But the line between the two was often hard to draw and many civilians and their lawyers chose not to recognize the distinction.[11] They asked that, before they disbanded, they should receive security for their arrears of pay; for provision for maimed soldiers, widows and orphans; and that those who had volunteered should not be forced to serve abroad. These were not radical demands, and were confined to the soldiers' professional interests, as soldiers: there was no hint of political or religious demands.[12] The tone was respectful throughout, and the whole document was based on the assumption that the army was to be disbanded or sent to Ireland. This moderation may have reflected the influence of the officers, but there can be little doubt that the petition expressed the sense of the great majority of officers and men in the New Model.

To respond to the petition as the Presbyterians in the Commons did was tactless and provocative in the extreme, especially as the House had welcomed petitions from London (again) and Essex, which claimed that the New Model wished to overawe Parliament and called for its disbandment. The soldiers were incensed that after all they had been through for the service of Parliament they should be publicly denounced as enemies of the state and disturbers of the public peace. As the news spread, officers and men alike expressed outrage at this affront to the army's honour and called for the Declaration of Dislike to be withdrawn, and those responsible for it to be punished. (It had, in fact, been drafted by Holles.) The Presbyterians, alarmed, tried to hurry up the process of enlistment for Ireland and the disbandment of the remainder of the army. They tried to drive a wedge between officers and men and to rendezvous regiments separately. But the men of most regiments were determined to maintain their solidarity. Regiments were scattered across much of the south-east, but communication between them was brisk, assisted by the press. A minority of officers volunteered for Ireland, but often these could not persuade their men to follow them. Fairfax and the senior officers were ordered to clamp down on this ferment of discussion. They gave the appearance of trying to do so, but some sympathized with the men and many of the regimental officers (colonels downwards) actively promoted the process of consultation. Opposition to the Irish service grew and there were increasingly insistent calls for a general rendezvous, where the army as a whole could discuss the situation.

The Commons and the Derby House Committee became alarmed. They began to offer concessions: the soldiers were offered some of their arrears and a partial indemnity. Later Parliament established an indemnity committee, which was intended to remove cases involving soldiers from the courts and so protect them against the vengeance of civilians. (However, the committee had heard only eighty-six cases by November 1647.)[13] But the Presbyterians, encouraged by their brethren in London, also tried to build up a military force of their own, to protect them against the army. This was to be based on the City-trained bands, over which the City regained control in April, and disbanded soldiers ('reformadoes') who thronged the City, demanding their arrears. These reformadoes were officers who were supposed to serve in the ranks, and they were notoriously unruly – 'a rabble of gentility'.[14] There were also hopes of enlisting support from the remainder of the Northern army, the Scots and those of the New Model who had volunteered for Ireland. If these were ever to be welded into one force, it would be a motley body and there were large question marks over several of its constituent elements. But the prospect of it gave the Presbyterians renewed, if perhaps exaggerated, confidence.

The army saw the creation of this 'alternative army' as a direct threat; it called for it to be disbanded and those responsible for raising it to be punished. There were also steps to formalize the process of consultation within the army. In the New Model strict discipline proved compatible with a culture of consultation, reinforced by seeking God together in prayer meetings. In councils of war (which involved only officers) the most junior officers gave their opinions first and the most senior at the end, so that juniors would not be influenced by the views of their seniors. In April the soldiers of eight cavalry regiments chose commissioners, who became known as adjutators,

agitators or agents (meaning one who acts on behalf of others).
It is probably pointless to ask whether the initiative for this
came from the officers or the rank and file. The latter certainly
formed their own organization and acquired their own printing
presses, to counter what they saw as misrepresentation; they
had a strong sense of being undervalued and insulted, especially
by the Declaration of Dislike. They also showed themselves
quite capable of defying officers who volunteered for Ireland
and tried to persuade them to do the same.

On 3 May an 'apology' of the soldiers urged the officers to
stand by their men in defence of the liberties of the subject: it
was better to die fighting than to submit to slavery.[15] The only
specific complaint in the 'apology' was the punishment of
soldiers for actions while in Parliament's service, but ten days
later some regiments raised other issues, including liberty of
conscience, the right to petition Parliament, and the injustice of
having the laws in an unknown tongue.[16] The last was a long-
standing grievance of the Levellers. These[17] and London
radicals, who had hitherto viewed the army with suspicion and
even hostility, watched its growing resentment with interest. If
the army could be persuaded to adopt a form of Leveller
programme, it was far more likely to succeed than if the
Levellers stuck to their usual tactic of petitioning an unre-
sponsive Parliament. They urged the soldiers to broaden their
demands, but initially the soldiers were wary of going beyond
their professional grievances.[18] There is no reason to suspect
that these concerns were not shared by many officers. There
was an overwhelming opposition among the soldiers to serving
in Ireland and the great majority of the officers stayed with
their men.[19] Presbyterian officers were isolated and vilified.
This was, moreover, an army that had developed an exceptional
solidarity, which knew that it could achieve its aims only if it
maintained unity. And some of those aims were shared
throughout the army: a vindication of its honour; an indemnity;
and full arrears of pay. Towards the end of May the Derby
House Committee made one last attempt to drive a wedge

between the cavalry and infantry, officers and men. It planned to disband all the infantry at once, and to recruit reformadoes in their places. At the same time the Commons voted extra money for the London-trained bands. The effect of the Committee's hardline attitude was to stiffen the army's determination: the agitators called for a general rendezvous of the whole army, to discuss its next move. The council of war agreed: a general rendezvous would make the army able to resist disbandment as fiercely as a bear protecting her cubs.[20] 'Provocation and exasperation makes men think of what they never intended.'[21]

The confrontation between Parliament and army came to a head in early June. On the 3rd a junior officer, Cornet Joyce, seized the king, who was under genteel house arrest at Holdenby House in Northamptonshire. Charles had been engaged in lengthy and desultory negotiations with the Presbyterians, which had foundered on the question of episcopacy. He had also been involved in clandestine discussions with one faction of the Scots, and others. He seemed quite content to be seized: being taken to the army offered yet more opportunities to play one group off against another. He was pleased that his captors treated him with courtesy and allowed him the services of his chaplains, denied him by the Scots and the Presbyterians. He raised no objection to being taken to the main body of the army at Newmarket. It seems probable that Cromwell and others of the high command knew about Joyce's mission, but found it prudent not to admit this publicly. Cromwell certainly approved a move to change the king's guards at Holdenby, as he had heard of a plan to move the king elsewhere, but he does not seem to have sanctioned taking possession of the king's person.

The significance of the move was obvious. As the soldiers pondered on their maltreatment by Parliament, it was natural that they should try to explain what they saw as the Presbyterians' haughty and morally odious behaviour. It would not be surprising if they came up with answers similar to those advanced by Leveller pamphlets: that too long an enjoyment of power had corrupted them. Just as they began to understand their own position in wider political terms, so they began to see that their grievances could be satisfactorily resolved only as part of a wider political settlement. A year after the end of the war there had still been no settlement with the king. The army's friends in Parliament, the Independents, blamed this on the Presbyterians' intransigence, especially on the question of bishops. One way of getting round the stalemate that this had caused was for the army to try to negotiate a settlement with him instead; and for that it needed access to his person. The courtesy with which he was treated suggested that at this stage the army felt little or no hostility towards his person and no lasting rancour towards the Royalists. As Fairfax was to remark in July: 'We think that tender, equitable and moderate dealing, both towards His Majesty, his royal family and his late party . . . is the most hopeful course to take away the seeds of war.'[22] And if a settlement with the king included some checks on the misuse of power by Parliament, so much the better.

Meanwhile, there was a general rendezvous of the army near Newmarket on 4 and 5 June. This approved a 'Solemn Engagement', in which the army resolved to disband only when its grievances were met. These included the withdrawal of the Declaration of Dislike, the granting of a full indemnity and the punishment of those most active against the army. The Engagement was probably drawn up mainly by Cromwell's son-in-law, Commissary-General Henry Ireton, probably in consultation with some of the agitators.[23] Meanwhile, the agitators, two from every regiment, were invited to form part of a General Council of the Army, along with two officers from each regiment and the generals and some members of their staff. The General Council could be summoned only by Fairfax, and the presence of the general staff meant that there was a built-in majority of officers, but a significant number of officers, senior and junior, were at least as radical as the rank and file, and tended to speak more often in debate. The real point of the General Council was that it greatly speeded the process of consultation. Moreover, its representative nature gave it a real claim to speak for the army as a whole. The agitators do not seem to think that the General Council was designed to manipulate or control them: indeed, there was a real sense of cooperation and unity.

Parliament's attempts to break the unity of the army had failed. It showed its alarm at the events of 3 to 5 June by expunging the Declaration of Dislike from the Commons Journal and granting a full and unqualified indemnity. The City, equally alarmed, sent a deputation to negotiate with the army. The army then began to march ominously towards London. On 14 June its first manifesto, an explanation of the Solemn Engagement, was drawn up by Ireton and others at St Alban's, and approved by a council of war (which consisted only of officers). This document, 'A Declaration or Representation', firmly placed the grievances of the army in the wider context of the grievances of the nation.[24] It claimed a right to propose measures designed to settle the kingdom and to achieve the ends for which the war had been fought. It stated resoundingly: 'we were not a mere mercenary army, hired to serve any arbitrary power of a state, but called forth and conjured by the several declarations of Parliament to the defence of our own and the people's just rights and liberties'. They had taken up arms 'in judgement and conscience' against all arbitrary power whatsoever.[25] The Declaration called for the removal from Parliament of those guilty of corruption and those responsible for 'unjust and high proceedings' against the army. It then set out its proposals. A date should be fixed for the end of this Parliament, with measures to ensure regular Parliaments in future. The electoral system should be made more equitable, with constituencies of roughly equal size: at present large counties such as Yorkshire elected as many members (two) as tiny and decayed Cornish boroughs. Frequent and fairer elections would together make the Commons more answerable to the people; the powers of Parliaments should also be defined and limited and there should be an end to the arbitrary powers of county committees. Steps should be taken to prevent undue dissolutions by the king, or Parliaments sitting too long. The Declaration also called for a vindication of the subject's right to petition and a guarantee of liberty for persons with tender consciences, provided they lived soberly and peaceably.

This was hardly an elaborate constitutional blueprint, and included many items of particular interest to the army, including a call for indemnity and proper accounting by those who had handled public money. But it did assert the army's right to engage in politics and the principle that Parliaments as well as kings needed to be curbed. And there was the call for liberty for tender consciences. A much more fully worked out constitutional proposal was drawn up by the army command, probably in consultation with the Parliamentary Independents, and presented to the king in July. Some provisions dealt with restrictions on the king. His negative voice (veto over legislation) was to be limited. The militia was to be controlled by a new executive committee, the council of state, for ten years. Parliament was to approve the choice of ministers and officers, also for ten years. After the ten years were up, the king was to regain command of the armed forces and partial control over the appointment of ministers and officers. There was to be widespread freedom of worship, including for those using the Prayer Book; bishops could be restored, so long as they had no coercive powers over those who wished to opt out of the national church. There were to be biennial parliamentary elections; seats were to be redistributed on the basis of taxes paid.

These 'Heads of the Proposals' were the most favourable terms that the king received. The provisions about elections showed that they were concerned to limit Parliament as well as the king. He was not to be permanently deprived of his core prerogatives and he was to be allowed to have an episcopal church in which the Prayer Book could be used, provided that people could not be forced to attend its services. The proposals envisaged that the king would have some power (but not much) from the outset and significantly more after ten years. The generosity of the terms reflects partly the need to outbid the Presbyterians, partly a sense that Parliament was currently the more potent threat to the people's liberties, and partly the fact that those who drafted the Heads had no first-hand experience of dealing with the king: it was possible to blame the failure to reach a settlement so far on the stubbornness of the Presbyterians, rather than the obduracy of the king. Experience was to show that this was mistaken. Charles was happy to negotiate with the army leaders, but did not trust them: he remarked, with surprise, that they had not asked for favours for themselves, an interesting illustration of his views on political morality. He clung to his belief that they could not survive without him: 'I shall see them glad ere long to accept more equal terms.'[26] Convinced that he could get an even better offer elsewhere, Charles turned down the Heads on 28 July. He objected in particular to the suggestion that any of the Royalists should be excluded from pardon and insisted that the Church should be established by law.[27] As an expression of its frustration, the General Council adopted the Heads as the official army programme. They were printed, to show the public what the king had rejected.

Although Parliament now seemed prepared to meet the army's professional demands, this was no longer enough, now that the army had begun to formulate a political programme. On 16 July, at Reading, the General Council debated how far the army should put pressure on Parliament to meet its immediate demands (the high command had yet to put its proposals for a general settlement to the king). These demands included the removal of eleven MPs deemed by the army to be responsible for the Declaration of Dislike and the organization of the 'alternative army'; changes in the London militia committee, to remove it from Presbyterian control; and the release from prison of John Lilburne and other London radicals.[28] Lilburne was one of the leading Levellers, a charismatic but wayward figure, who seemed to court persecution and punishment. His sheer cussedness made him popular even among people who did not share his views, but he was also a man who harboured strong enmities and possessed a vitriolic pen. The fact that the General Council called for his release is an indication of Leveller influence in the army; the fact that Lilburne soon developed a fierce hatred of Cromwell and other 'grandees' (members of the high command) would threaten to turn the soldiers against their leaders. (The Levellers did not attack Fairfax, whose popularity with his men placed him above criticism.) For the moment, however, Lilburne remained in gaol, and the General Council, after considerable debate, resolved not to march on London. To those who argued that the army's consistent success thus far showed that it was God's chosen instrument, Cromwell replied that they needed to wait for a clear indication of God's will, as manifested in events. It would also be prudent to wait on the outcome of the negotiations with the king.

While these negotiations were continuing, a dramatic turn of events, of the sort that Cromwell was waiting for, did indeed occur. Both Parliament and the City had responded to the army's public statements and its advance towards the City with a mixture of defiance and fear. On 11 June the Commons committee for Irish affairs resolved to appoint a committee of safety to raise forces to oppose the army, with a particular brief to recruit reformadoes; but men came in slowly, especially as the army moved closer. The City had been glad to regain their old (Presbyterian-controlled) militia committee, but many citizens had proved unwilling to serve and even refused to obey their Presbyterian officers. Faced with the army's demands from Reading, the Commons handed the London militia committee back to the Independents, but some Londoners, fearful of a possible deal between the king and the army, believed that this was the last chance for Parliament and the City to take a stand, especially as the Commons were inclined to be conciliatory. On 26 July the common council marched to Westminster to demand that control of the militia be handed back to the City; the newly reinstated Independent militia committee was ejected by force. The council was accompanied by a large crowd of apprentices and others, who bullied the few peers in the Lords into passing an ordinance to reinstate the Presbyterian militia committee, and then invaded the Commons and demanded that the Lower House follow suit. Faced with resistance they became abusive and violent, throwing excrement in members' faces. Eventually the House voted to restore the militia committee and to invite the king to London, with apprentices sitting among the members and joining in the votes.[29]

There was no doubt that some of the common council and at least one alderman not only connived at the riot but actively organized it. The lord mayor refused to send the trained bands to protect the Houses and some Presbyterian MPs knew what was intended. After their frightening ordeal, numerous members of both Houses, including the speakers, fled to the army for safety; others stayed away from Westminster. Those who remained, overwhelmingly Presbyterians, passed a series of defiantly partisan measures and tried to organize the 'alternative army' based on the militia, reformadoes and men who had left the New Model. For a few days the grandees were preoccupied with their negotiations with the king, but retribution was not long in coming. On 3 August the army entered the City. After all its bravado, the common council's resolution vanished. The City trained bands were deeply divided about the feasibility of opposing the army, and resistance quickly collapsed. Many citizens welcomed the soldiers, who by the end of the 4th controlled the City. On the 7th the regiments mustered in Hyde Park and then marched in smaller units through every part of the City – at once a show of force, but also a demonstration of the New Model's discipline.[30] The Independent MPs and the two speakers returned in triumph; the militia committee changed yet again. The Presbyterians in the Commons were not completely cowed. Not until 20 August did the Commons agree to expel the eleven members, or to annul the measures passed in the absence of the Independents; it did so then only after 1,000 soldiers had been drawn up in Hyde Park and both officer-MPs and officers around the House had warned of the dangers of defiance.[31] Nevertheless, an important lesson had been learned. The army had shown that it was prepared to use force to coerce Parliament, and the Presbyterians' much-vaunted 'alternative army' had proved no match for the New Model. Just to reinforce the message, the army ordered the destruction of the City's fortifications, built at such enormous effort in 1643. The army also established its headquarters much closer to London, at Putney. But at this stage the army had no wish to subject Parliament to sustained military pressure. The grandees hoped that, with the Presbyterians suitably chastened, and the eleven trouble-makers removed, they would now be able to work with Parliament.

After the march on London, it was clear that the army had the power to impose its will on Parliament, if it so chose. For the moment, the grandees, several of whom were MPs, did not so choose. They preferred, on principle, to work with Parliament, and there was the very practical consideration that the army needed Parliament to vote its pay and, through its indemnity committee, to protect soldiers against prosecution for their past actions. It was unfortunate that Parliament was slow to vote the necessary money, leading to suspicions that it wished to force the army to take free quarter and so render it even more unpopular. Others in the army were less inhibited. Since the Declaration of 14 June the army was committed to bringing about a political settlement that would secure the liberties of the people, and there was naturally much discussion about how this could be done. Increasingly, this discussion was influenced by the Levellers, who had begun to think about such matters much earlier, in the context of their disillusionment with 'parliamentary tyranny'. The Levellers argued that MPs had to be made truly answerable to the people, through frequent, regular elections and a more equitable electoral system. At this stage they seemed to be concerned less with the franchise than with the redistribution of seats; constituencies varied enormously in size, with the number of electors ranging from around a dozen to several thousand. The Levellers had repeatedly called on Parliament to bring itself to an end and hold fresh elections, using a reformed electoral system. For this system to be effective, and to prevent these changes from being reversed in future, the provision for regular elections should be made into 'laws paramount', or fundamental laws, which once enacted could not be revoked. Some also proposed other laws paramount, including a guarantee of liberty of conscience.

It is understandable that many in the army would have found these proposals attractive. They had had ample experience of parliamentary bullying and bluster, and were frustrated that, after the king's refusal to agree to the Heads of the Proposals, the grandees seemed in no hurry to proceed to a political settlement. The Levellers and many in the army believed that the removal of the eleven members did not go far enough: corruption was far more deeply rooted than that. There were calls to remove all who had sat in Parliament between 26 July and 6 August, which would have purged the Houses of committed Presbyterians and given the Independents free rein. With most army units stationed not far from London, contacts between army and Levellers became more frequent. The Levellers, for their part, believed that the army could bring Parliament to agree to the changes that they demanded far more quickly than any number of petitions. They saw the grandees as the main obstacle they faced and tried to incite the rank and file (and more radical officers) to put pressure on the grandees. The differences between the grandees and the Levellers rested less on their respective programmes – those parts of the Heads of the Proposals which dealt with Parliament were quite similar to Leveller proposals – than on their willingness to take decisive, and possibly violent, action to bring them about. Meanwhile, as their pay continued heavily in arrears, the soldiers were encouraged to blame the grandees for not looking after their interests.

And then there was the question of the king. For a few brief days in July the grandees had been prepared to offer him terms even more generous than the Heads of the Proposals, but Charles turned the offer down, in the hope of a better one from someone else. Nevertheless, negotiations with the king continued. Charles continued to hope that he could be restored without the army, but in September he said he preferred the Heads to Parliament's proposals and wished Parliament would consider them. First-hand experience of dealing with the king turned some of the senior officers against him, and this anger and frustration spread through the army. The king's refusal to come to terms after his defeat in 1646 had left his erstwhile opponents with two possible choices. Either they could settle with the king on terms which he was prepared to accept, which would mean abandoning all that the civil war had been fought for; or they could reach a settlement without him. Both were unthinkable, so they did what people normally do in such circumstances: they kept on and on negotiating, hoping that, sooner or later, something would turn up. But in the second half of 1647 some in the army and elsewhere began to think the unthinkable, to argue that the king was the main obstacle to a settlement and that he was incorrigible and deserving of condign punishment. Such views were confined to a small minority at the time, but that minority was to grow. As it did so, and became more vociferous, the moderates in Parliament became more and more alarmed, ready to settle with the king on almost any terms. That stage had not yet been reached in 1647, but dissatisfaction within the army was reaching levels that seriously worried the grandees. On the other hand, the Levellers were disappointed that they could not persuade the agitators to adopt their constitutional programme. As a consequence, in late September 'new agitators' appeared, who claimed to represent five regiments, and later another six. It is not clear how far they really did, but some seem to have been elected.[32] They stayed in London, not with the army, and worked closely with the Levellers and other London radicals. If these marked the start of a plan to erect a new General Council, independent of the grandees, it was ominous. Something needed to be done, to remove this threat and reinforce the authority of the high command.

This could not be done by simply issuing orders and demanding compliance: that was not the army's way. All through its rise to political prominence the army had maintained its habit of consultation, exemplified not only in the General Council but also in mass prayer meetings. This was also essential to maintain its unity. It had many enemies. The majority in the Commons was cowed but resentful, and it remained deeply unpopular among the people at large, because of the financial burden it imposed, because of its religious extremism, and because of its growing habit of ordering around the rulers and inhabitants of the towns where it was quartered. The differences of opinion within the army needed to be addressed and discussed, and the proper venue for this was the General Council, which met at the army's headquarters at Putney at the end of October. To allow the army radicals' civilian friends to have their say, a small group of them were invited to take part in what was otherwise an internal army discussion, and as such the proceedings were private. If we now know a lot about what was said, this is because the secretary to the General Council, William Clarke, took shorthand notes on the proceedings of three days of the debates. But these proceedings were not widely known at the time and Clarke's notes lay buried in his papers at Worcester College, Oxford, until the end of the nineteenth century.

The Putney debates lasted from 28 October until 9 November. On the first day the civilian Levellers produced a draft Agreement of the People, a short document, which gives the impression of having been thrown together hurriedly. It called for the current Parliament to dissolve itself by 30 September 1648 and then to hold elections every two years, using constituencies that were approximately equal in terms of population. It set out certain fundamentals which future Parliaments could not change: liberty of conscience, equality before the law, a ban on conscription and a general indemnity for things said or done during 'the late public differences'.[33] This was a limited programme, and there was much in it that the grandees could accept. Indeed, those who presented the Agreement stressed that much of it was already present in the Declaration of 14 June.[34] On the other hand, it was not clear how Parliament could be brought to accept the Agreement, other than by force. The Heads of the Proposals had committed the army to constitutional means: any settlement should be implemented by Parliament.[35] And the Heads of the Proposals, endorsed by the General Council as the army's official programme, had made no mention of unalterable fundamentals. The Agreement made no reference to the king or House of Lords. At Cromwell's suggestion, a committee was appointed to consider how far the Agreement was compatible with the army's engagements (in other words, the declaration of 14 June and the Heads of the Proposals). The committee included both a leading London Leveller, Richard Overton, and prominent army radicals.

Next day, after a lengthy prayer meeting, Cromwell's son-in-law, General Henry Ireton, returned to the Agreement. He noted that it stated that in future parliamentary constituencies should be based on population, whereas the Heads had stated that it should be made on the basis of taxes paid. He expressed concern that this implied that people should be represented in the Commons, rather than property. Did this mean that those without property would be able to vote, and might they not use their superior numbers to deprive the propertied of their property? The responses to his speech suggested that no one had thought much about the franchise, and the main concern, in both the Heads and the Agreement, had been to demand more equal constituencies. Responses varied. Lieutenant Colonel Thomas Rainsborough came out unequivocally for universal adult male suffrage: 'Every man that is to live under a government ought first by his own consent to put himself under that government.' This applied as much to the 'poorest he' as to the 'greatest he'.[36] Others, such as the civilian radical Maximilian Petty, argued that the vote should go to those who could use it independently – in other words, not servants, or those receiving poor relief, or wage labourers. The debate that Ireton triggered was in some ways a diversion, and soured the atmosphere: whatever the Levellers stood for, it was not the levelling of property. Indeed, there seemed little point in reopening the question of the Agreement, which had already been referred to a committee. This produced a set of proposals fuller than those set out in the Agreement. It quietly omitted the idea of a written constitution endorsed by the people, but included a list of fundamentals that Parliament could not alter – the right to freedom of conscience, freedom from impressment for service abroad, and an indemnity for the soldiers. It agreed that Parliament should dissolve itself by 1 September 1648 and make provision for biennial Parliaments, which were to sit for no longer than six months. Parliament was to decide on the franchise and how seats were to be redistributed. Much of the business of the executive was to be handled by a council of state, present in the Heads, but not in the Agreement: the Levellers never really concerned themselves with the executive, or practical questions of how government was to be carried on. It was assumed that both the monarchy and the Lords should continue, but with reduced power. The whole package was to be submitted to Parliament for its approval.[37]

Despite the ill-feeling caused by Ireton on the question of the franchise, the committee's report represented a reasonable attempt to find common ground. The Levellers, two days before the report of the committee on the Agreement, printed it, claiming that it was the sense of the army, and there were further attacks in print on Cromwell and Ireton. The General Council was irritated by this sharp practice, but the Agreement was not the most contentious issue at Putney. More significant was the question of who was to control the army. London radicals attacked the grandees in the press, the rank and file were restive, and within the General Council there were moves to reduce their authority within the army as a whole. These moves never amounted to an overt challenge to the grandees, and did not succeed, but they added to the grandees' unease. But the most contentious issue, if not the best reported, was that of the king. Well before Putney there were some, like the civilian Leveller John Wildman, who described the king as a 'man of blood' who should be brought to trial and punished. On 1 November there was an angry row about whether the king should have a reduced negative voice, as stated in the Heads; many thought he should have none at all. The committee that examined the Agreement did not include in its report the provisions in the Heads that the king should be deprived of his control over his ministers and the armed forces for ten years only; this was not likely to go down well with the General Council in its current mood.

On 5 November, the day the committee reported, it was voted by a narrow margin to write to Parliament to demand that it should make no further approaches to the king. Ireton, always irascible, stormed out. The issue came up again on the 9th, when many of those present condemned this vote; however, Colonel Thomas Harrison declared that the king should be executed, and he had his supporters among the agitators. The grandees had already decided that enough was enough: there would clearly be no agreement on the terms to put to the king and the open hostility towards him needed to be nipped in the bud. There was general unease at the divisions within the army and resentment of the attempts by the London radicals and their allies in the army to incite the soldiers to mutiny.[38] When Fairfax ordered the agitators back to their regiments, the General Council seems to have concurred.

Fairfax was far less of a politician than Cromwell or Ireton, but he was an experienced soldier with a good military record and a reputation for looking after his men, who trusted him. He ordered three separate rendezvous, judging that it would be unwise to have the whole army in one place, and announced that he would address each regiment in turn. The Levellers tried to whip up the soldiers to defy their officers, and a few regiments were mutinous. This was not necessarily as a result of Leveller agitation. Some days before the rendezvous were ordered, Colonel Robert Lilburne's regiment had refused to obey an order to march north, fearing that if it did so the men would not receive the pay promised them by Parliament. Both Levellers and Royalists tried to stir up the men: the latter were apparently more successful, as 400 soldiers resolved to bring the king back to Whitehall. When their officers refused to join them, they 'discharged' them. In the fracas that followed, two soldiers were killed and an officer had his hand cut off. The regiment, with only one junior officer, Lieutenant Bray, wandered around the countryside, plundering the people and searching for 'roundheads', and eventually turned up unbidden at the first rendezvous, at Ware, expecting to receive its pay.[39] A second regiment, Harrison's, also turned up unbidden, without its colonel and most of its officers. Here Leveller influence was more apparent, and the soldiers had copies of the Agreement of the People in their hats. Leveller sympathizers among the officers urged the men to demand that the army adopt the Agreement. Fairfax ordered them from the field and Cromwell and Ireton began to remove the papers from the men's hats. Seeing that the other soldiers did not join them, the rest of the regiment removed the papers voluntarily. Lilburne's regiment arrived late in the proceedings, also with copies of the Agreement in their hats, but some of the soldiers complained that an officer who tried to bring them to order was against the king, and the soldiers began to throw stones at him; it seems that the soldiers of this regiment had completely lost the plot. Again Cromwell and Ireton took the lead in removing the papers. Fairfax made a brief speech to each regiment, and Cromwell and Ireton put forward a 'remonstrance'. This blamed a small minority of trouble-makers for trying to divide the army (Fairfax blamed the London agents). The remonstrance promised redress of the soldiers' practical and professional grievances, the dissolution of this Parliament, regular Parliaments in future, and free and equal elections, 'to render the House of Commons (as near as may be) an equal representative of the people'. Each regiment was to subscribe the remonstrance, to show the soldiers' agreement and their obedience to Fairfax and the General Council; the remonstrance thus became the army's official manifesto and engagement. For most of the soldiers this was enough and they waved their hats and cried 'for the king and Sir Thomas'.[40]

Fairfax did not wish to punish severely those responsible for the disorders at Ware; after the recent divisions and recrimination, there was a need to restore unity. He believed that most had been misled, but now saw the error of their ways. Lieutenant Bray and those who had tried to persuade the men to adopt the Agreement were court martialled, but were later pardoned after humbly confessing their fault. On the other hand, the mutiny in Lilburne's regiment could not be allowed to go unpunished. Eleven ringleaders were sentenced to death. Fairfax reduced the number to three, of whom one was shot by the other two. Order and discipline were restored with apparent ease. The grandees had given the Levellers and their army allies a hearing, but the General Council had refused to adopt their programme, and the grandees emerged with their authority enhanced. If the Levellers had seriously hoped to take over the army and use it to implement their programme, they had failed. This owed something to the grandees' resolute action after Putney, but more to the army's unity and solidarity. During the remainder of 1647, the grandees tightened their control. In December they demanded that Parliament should make proper financial provision for the army: since their proposals included paying off some 20,000 men, out of

44,000, Parliament was not reluctant to comply. The reductions offered the chance to weed out some of the more disruptive, or less effective, elements, including the former Royalists, the remaining Presbyterians and the Leveller sympathizers. The New Model emerged from this exercise leaner and fitter, and eager to restore its unity. It held a ten-hour 'day of humiliation', in which the officers and men sought God together; it ended with a symbolic gesture of forgiveness and reconciliation – the abandonment of proceedings against two officers charged with mutiny.[41] The army was to need all its solidarity in the coming year.

8

PRIDE'S PURGE

With its unity largely restored, Parliament seemingly amenable and London apparently cowed, the main threats to the army came from elsewhere. The events of 1647, and especially the march on London, had increased popular hostility to the army still further. The army was now an intrusive presence in the many garrison towns, promoting godly reform and pressing for, or ordering, the removal of the allegedly disaffected from municipal office. The assessment was reorganized and became, if anything, even more burdensome; soldiers were quartered on those who failed to pay. Parliament was slow to provide money for the army, and many of the soldiers who were supposed to have been disbanded remained in arms and continued to demand free quarter, which had been forbidden by Parliament in December 1647. The replacement of well-loved pastors by godly outsiders caused resentment and sometimes violence, and there were riots in six counties against the prohibition of Christmas and others against attempts to enforce sabbath observance. London was in fact less cowed than it seemed: early 1648 saw a virtual tax strike and increasingly open Royalist demonstrations. For popular hostility to the army was increasingly expressed in terms of Royalism, and there were strident calls to Parliament to settle with the king on almost any terms, or even unconditionally. The majority in Parliament, although fearful of provoking the army's wrath, was increasingly to sympathize with these demands: almost anything was better than being pushed around by the army.

The major source of the army's problems was the king. Two days after the Putney debates broke up, Charles escaped from Hampton Court. It seems possible that this was connected to the hostility shown towards him at Putney, but his departure caused anger among the high command because he had renounced his parole. Having tried unsuccessfully to flee the country, he ended up in Carisbrooke Castle on the Isle of Wight in the custody of Colonel Robert Hammond, Cromwell's nephew; Hammond's brother, Henry, was one of the king's favourite clergymen. Hammond was deeply unhappy about his role as the king's gaoler, and asked repeatedly to be relieved of the responsibility; Charles was not an easy prisoner and tried several times to escape. Charles was soon negotiating with a group of Scottish nobles. Quite how he was able to continue these negotiations is unclear: Scots would presumably be somewhat conspicuous on the Isle of Wight – and the king was supposed to be a prisoner. On 26 December he and these Scots signed the Engagement, under which the Scots would bring an army into England to restore the king's powers in full. In this document, the army was accused of carrying the king away from Holdenby against his will, and using force against Parliament, and the Scots undertook to bring Charles to London, where he could negotiate in person with Parliament. In return, he agreed to establish Presbyterianism in England for three years and to promote an Act of Parliament to suppress the sects.[1]

This was an agreement reflecting desperation on both sides. The king knew he had the support of much of England's population, but the latest proposals he had received from Parliament were totally unacceptable, since they took as their starting point that he should be deprived permanently of control over the armed forces. The mood of Parliament could change; a much bigger problem was how to overcome the army. Charles had been totally defeated in England and could hope, at best, that some of his English subjects would rise up if a Scots army came to challenge the New Model. He could expect no significant assistance from Ireland, where a Parliamentary force had inflicted a serious defeat on the Confederate Catholics. As for the Scots, the Covenanters were now deeply divided. Those who signed the Engagement did so as leaders of a faction, not a nation. The Engagement was fiercely opposed by the clergy and a significant section of the nobility, and not without reason. Establishing Presbyterianism for only three years seemed totally impractical; the only indication of what would happen when the three years were over was that the question of future church government was to be referred to an assembly of divines from England and Scotland, a recipe for inconclusive wrangling. The strong opposition to the Engagement in Scotland would ensure that the Engagers' military preparations were both slow and inadequate and their army entered England only in July.

News of the Engagement was greeted with outrage in Parliament. The Independents were particularly incensed, but many others saw it as yet further evidence of the king's bad faith – especially as the king had agreed to the Engagement rather than Parliament's own recent proposals. On 3 January the Commons resolved by a significant majority that no further proposals should be made to the king (the Vote of No Addresses). Several urged that the kingdom should be settled without the king and one MP called for him to be impeached. The vehemence of the Commons alarmed some of the peers and the Lords delayed for a week considering the Vote, eventually approving it on 17 January, only too aware that they were under close scrutiny from two regiments quartered at Westminster. Not surprisingly, the army agreed with the Vote.

The General Council, in its last meeting, declared that there was no hope of reaching a settlement through negotiations with the king and that Parliament should consider securing itself and the kingdom 'without the king and against him'.[2] A similar hardening can be seen in the administrative sphere. The Derby House Committee was now dominated by the Independents; its decision-making power grew at the expense of the two Houses. But if the army's friends controlled the government, its enemies became increasingly vociferous. The Christmas riots showed how isolated and unpopular they were. The mayor of Canterbury refused to mark the day even with a sermon and ordered shopkeepers to keep their shops open; those who did so were violently attacked and their shops looted. The riot began with a football match, which the mayor had forbidden, and developed into a general attack on the ministers and magistrates. The mayor and sheriff were badly beaten up, dragged home and forced to provide free drink for all comers. Next day the rioters were joined by others from the neighbouring villages. They seized the city magazine and the weapons kept in the town hall, and controlled access to the city. After a few days, however, they surrendered to the Kent militia. Even a packed grand jury refused to find that the rioters had a case to answer, so the county committee asked the Commons if they could be tried by martial law.[3]

The Canterbury riots showed how easily political protests or riots could slide into something like insurrection. On 27 March, the king's accession day, there were scores of bonfires in London – more than in any year since the king's accession. Robert Hammond was burned in effigy and the gates had to be shut to stop the crowds marching to Westminster. Londoners, so hostile to the army in 1646–7, had been severely shocked by the army's march into the City in August 1647, but were now beginning to recover their nerve. On Sunday 9 April a crowd of young men gathered in Moorfields to play tipcat. They had been forbidden to play the previous Sunday by the 'godly' lord mayor and were in an angry mood. When the trained bands came to disperse them they were overpowered. The crowd marched down Fleet Street chanting 'Now for king Charles'. They were dispersed by the army, but gathered again the next day, attacked the lord mayor's house and forced him to take refuge in the Tower. The crowds were eventually dispersed by New Model cavalry: several were killed.[4] For much of 1648 the army was hard put to maintain some sort of control over London: the trained bands could no longer cope. In Norwich the mayor allowed coronation day to be celebrated. He was summoned to answer to Parliament, but refused to go. A demonstration in his favour ended with the crowd seizing the headquarters of the county committee, which was also the magazine. When troops arrived to restore order the magazine blew up, killing at least a hundred people.[5] There was similar defiance of Puritan authority elsewhere – a bull-baiting in Bath, a maypole at Bury St Edmund's. Plans to put the king's second son on the throne in his place – the eldest was abroad – were thwarted when he escaped to Holland in disguise. Most of the navy defected to Holland on the news that Rainsborough had been appointed its commander-in-chief. Unfortunately for the king, prince Charles's advisers could not agree what to do with it, and the opportunity of seriously embarrassing an already beleaguered regime was wasted. The prince cruised up and down the east coast and even into the Thames estuary, but made no significant contribution to the insurrections.

By April the extent of disaffection became still more apparent, with protests by grand juries and resistance to, and occasionally violence against, county committees. The most effective tactic of the opponents of Parliament and the army was the organization of mass petitions. What had once been the weapon of Parliamentary radicals had been appropriated by their enemies. These were in part a response to attempts by county committees to organize petitions expressing support for the Vote of No Addresses. One such attempt in Essex failed; a petition from Somerset was presented, amid accusations that people had been forced to subscribe by threats of sequestration. A rival petition from Essex, said to have 20,000 or even 30,000 signatures, was presented to Parliament by a crowd of 2,000 people, who were cheered through the streets on the way to Westminster. It called on Parliament to open negotiations with the king and disband the army. It was followed by another similar petition from Surrey, which had been adopted by a mass rally of freeholders and was accompanied to Westminster by 3,000 men. It led to scuffles in Parliament; when the soldiers guarding Parliament tried to disperse the crowd; a major fight developed in which ten people were killed. Subscriptions to petitions were also being gathered in other southern counties and numerous petitions were being drawn up in London. Although petitioning was a peaceful and lawful means of political action, the large crowds that accompanied the Essex and Surrey petitions were designed to show the strength of popular feeling and to intimidate Parliament. In May Parliament (which had welcomed mass petitions in 1640–2) passed an ordinance against 'tumultuous' petitioning, a striking testimony to its fear of the people.[6] This did not stop 10,000 Dorset men from subscribing to a 'declaration' in June, which called for the king to come to London. There should be a new, and genuinely representative, assembly of divines to settle church government. The existing MPs for the county, who had betrayed their trust, should be replaced by 'patriots', and the county committee should be replaced by the traditional officers, drawn from established county families. Those who had been sequestered for their loyalty should have their lands restored.[7] Throughout provincial England, and Wales, there was overwhelming evidence of dissatisfaction with the existing regime, and hatred for the army on which (however reluctantly) it depended.

The basic strategy agreed between the king and the Scots was that the Scottish army would be ready to invade England in May, at which time there would be several risings in different parts of the country. The New Model would have to send detachments to suppress these risings, leaving a reduced field army, which the Scots might hope to defeat, and take London, where support for the king was now so strong. But the Scots' military preparations took much longer than expected, and the planned risings took place before the Scots were ready. Nobody seems to have considered the possibility that neither the Royalists nor the Presbyterians would welcome the Scots. The Royalists were repelled by the king's willingness to deal with the Scots at all, and to sacrifice the Church; the Presbyterians were angry that he chose to come to terms with the Scots rather than with the English Parliament. The Scots, when they eventually came, made no friends, plundering Royalist and Parliamentarian alike during their brief time in northern England; in late 1648, of petitions calling for the king to be called to account, a disproportionately large number came from the North.

When the risings, which came to be known as the second civil war, began, those involved were a mixed bag, with disgruntled Parliamentarians (including former New Model soldiers), Royalists of varying degrees of extremism, and many who were simply fed up with county committees, crippling taxation and the burden of the military. The risings were not coordinated, so that the army did not have to deal with them all at the same time. The first, in South Wales, was checked by military defeat at St Fagan's on 8 May, but this was a region of strong castles and it took time to reduce them: Pembroke did not surrender until 11 July, at last freeing Cromwell and a section of the army to march north. As risings erupted in the provinces, London was seething with disaffection. Holles and two former Parliamentarian generals, Waller and Massey, were raising forces, and many Londoners were slipping away to join the disaffected in Kent and Essex. The Commons feared that London might be sliding out of control. To prevent this it appointed Major-General Philip Skippon commander-in-chief of the trained bands and all other forces in London. The City initially welcomed his appointment. He was a Presbyterian and widely regarded as a man of integrity, but he was to perform his task with ruthless efficiency. He ordered searches for arms and horses; many Royalist agents were arrested. He effectively encircled London with a series of forts and blockhouses, from Windsor to Romford, enabling the army to maintain a precarious order in the City. Once the various risings had been defeated, the army would be able to crush London's resistance once and for all.

The heavy-handed response to petitions from county committees, the army and Parliament helped convert protest into insurgency. Both Parliament and its local agents seemed authoritarian and out of touch with local opinion. By no means all this disaffection was Royalist, but Royalist slogans offered a means of annoying the regime, and the restoration of the king seemed the most likely way of bringing it to an end. Committed Royalists tried to channel this disaffection. It was most marked in Kent and Essex, two counties which had remained firmly under Parliament's control throughout the war; those of Royalist sympathies there had generally kept quiet. Kent was an exceptionally clannish county. The majority of the gentry married wives from other Kentish families, so that the landed elite was locked together by ties of kinship and friendship. The county committee was dominated by outsiders and was authoritarian and deeply unpopular, especially when it tried to suppress the county petition. 'On the one side you have a whole county, represented by all the knights, gentlemen and yeomen ... [and] a general and public unanimity ... On the other side you have about six or seven, or a few more, busy pragmatical committee men, having neither honour nor honesty, patronizing the separatists and sectaries ... [and] by them alone had in veneration.'[8] The ruling clique in Kent declared the Kentish petition seditious and tried to suppress it by force, using the militia, which made its promoters all the more determined to resist. Following a great meeting of the gentry on 21 May, some of the petitioners seized the magazine at Rochester. Next day many more of the gentry agreed to join and there was a plan to assemble on Blackheath, just to the south-east of London, on the 30th. The rising spread into the countryside, with gentlemen and their tenants taking up arms against the county committee and the army; other towns were secured, including Dartford. Royalists from Southwark secured Deptford. Some of those who took up arms later claimed that they had been pressured or threatened into doing so, or thought that they were simply supporting the petition. The insurgents were more than a match for the Kent militia, and it was a while before regular troops felt able to leave London. On 1 June the City government called for negotiations with the king, and a large assembly in Kent chose the earl of Holland to lead them; he suggested that the earl of Norwich should take charge instead. On the same day Skippon fortified London Bridge, to prevent Londoners from joining the insurgents, and Fairfax marched out to confront them. Some fell back into Maidstone, but Fairfax's superior tactical skills and the fighting qualities of his men told in a hard-fought encounter, and the town was taken. The main force of insurgents, under Norwich, remained intact, and marched to Blackheath, hoping to be welcomed by Londoners, but none appeared, and they dispersed. Many of the insurgents did not return home, however, but crossed the Thames into Essex, where another revolt was brewing.

The rising in Essex was more explicitly Royalist. Although it had seen no fighting in the first civil war, Royalist sentiment there had been strong. In Colchester, in particular, there had been bitter conflict in 1641–2 between the townspeople and the future Royalist Sir John Lucas, and a detachment from Colchester had played a part on the attacks on Catholics' houses in the Stour valley. The rising began on 4 June, when the county committee was seized at Chelmsford. Sir Charles Lucas, younger brother of Sir John (now Lord) Lucas, who had a commission from the prince of Wales to command the forces in the county, summoned the militia. He was an experienced soldier, and a local man; many of the militia agreed to serve under him, and they were joined by apprentices and watermen from London and many of the Kentish insurgents, still under the command of Norwich, including some who had acquitted themselves well at Maidstone. They were joined by Lord Capel, who had a commission from the prince to command in the whole of East Anglia. The Essex rising had abler commanders than that in Kent, but many remained loyal to Parliament and joined Fairfax's forces. The insurgents' strategy was to draw more forces out of London – Cromwell was down in South Wales with 8,000 men – in the hope that Londoners would then rise against the army; unlike the insurgents in Kent, they thought more in national than in local terms. This strategy depended on building up a sizeable force and keeping it in being. The insurgents managed to secure admittance into the well-fortified town of Colchester, which was promptly surrounded by New Model forces. The siege dragged on from June until August: the besiegers set out to starve the town into submission rather than risk storming it and being repulsed. The town sustained heavy damage – most of its churches were ruined – and the inhabitants suffered terrible privations. When it finally capitulated, the terms of surrender most unusually included the provision that some of the leaders of the defending forces should be executed. Lucas and Sir George Lisle were shot at Colchester; Capel was later beheaded, in London. A fine of £11,000 was imposed upon the exhausted townspeople. The second civil war was generally more brutal than the first. The Royalists in Colchester were accused of using bullets that had been roughened (to make a more dangerous wound) or poisoned. When the besieging soldiers broke into Lord Lucas's house, they were angry that there was nothing left to plunder, so they broke open the tombs of his wife and sister in the family vault, and dismembered them.[9]

The essentially local origins of the risings in South Wales, Kent and Essex helps explain their lack of coordination. The Welsh rising had been contained before that in Kent started, and that was over before a full-blown rising developed in Essex. Elsewhere there were riots rather than risings. Disaffection was most apparent in the south-east, which felt the influence of London, but was also the area where most of the New Model was stationed. Meanwhile, the preparations of Hamilton's Scottish army had taken much longer than anticipated, thanks mainly to the divisions among the Scottish nobility and clergy: many feared that renewed military intervention in England would invite reprisals from Parliament and the army. Hamilton's subordinates squabbled among themselves and questioned his judgement. When he eventually crossed into England on 8 July, the risings in the south-east were effectively over, apart from the siege of Colchester. The Scots' progress was slowed down by difficult terrain and unseasonably bad weather. Food and forage were scarce; the Scots forces were strung out over a distance of twenty miles. Their slow progress gave Cromwell time to bring his forces up from South Wales – they left only on 14 July. They too moved slowly: the men were hungry, many lacked shoes and stockings, and the roads were bad. The lack of proper clothing was made good en route, but it was not until 13 August that Cromwell linked up with Lambert, and the New Model's northern forces, in Yorkshire. The king and the Scots had hoped that many Royalists would come to join them: the North had been one of the most Royalist parts of the country in the first civil war. But few came: northern Royalists might be loyal to the king, but they hated the Scots, having endured three years of Scottish occupation during the first civil war, and Lancashire was the least Royalist county in the North of England. On 17 August Hamilton's bedraggled army was resoundingly defeated by Cromwell at Preston. Hamilton was caught with his forces on both sides of the River Ribble. It was a contest between the battle-hardened New Model and part of a demoralized, disoriented and hungry Scottish army; Cromwell's forces took almost 10,000 prisoners. For all practical purposes, the second civil war was over.

Reactions to the second civil war differed sharply. For the army and its godly allies it showed that the king and Royalists were incorrigible, determined to go on stirring up conflict. For those who saw Parliament's victory in the first civil war as God's righteous judgement on the Royalists it was worse than that: by refusing to accept God's verdict against them, they were guilty of a form of blasphemy. Starting the second civil war was not only a crime against the people but a crime against God. And crimes merited punishment. After each major episode, the leaders were put on trial before either a court martial or a high court of justice: much the same was to happen to defeated rebels in Ireland in 1649–52. Those who had surrendered and been given quarter in the first civil war were seen as especially guilty; many from South Wales and Colchester were transported to the West Indies. Parliament decreed that former Parliamentarian soldiers who took part in the risings were to be tried by martial law.

Of all the guilty Royalists, the guiltiest (of course) was the king, especially as he had tried to 'vassalize' England to a foreign power (the Scots). According to a story that first appeared in print a decade later, at a prayer meeting at Windsor on 29 April a section of the army had resolved to bring 'Charles Stuart, that man of blood' to an account for the blood that he had shed. This was not the first instance of the term 'man of blood' – as we have seen, John Wildman and Colonel Thomas Harrison had used it in 1647 – but its use at a prayer meeting showed that there was a growing sense in the army that Charles was guilty of bringing suffering and bloodshed to the nation. And for those steeped in the Old Testament, blood guilt could be expiated only by bloody punishment.[10] It is impossible to say how widespread this sense was within the army, but it is illuminating to read Cromwell's letter to the speaker of the Commons after his victory at Preston. Written in a mood of exaltation after the battle, Cromwell gave a detailed account of the fighting and then spelled out the lessons to be drawn from this victory. 'Surely', he wrote, 'this is nothing but the hand of God; and wherever anything in this world is exalted, or exalts itself, God will pull it down; for this is the day wherein He alone will be exalted.' He urged

Parliament to go on and do the work of God 'and not hate His people, who are as the apple of His eye, and for whom even kings shall be reproved'. Those who persisted in troubling the land should be 'destroyed out of the land' (which could imply exile rather than execution).[11]

This should not be taken to mean that Cromwell was convinced that the king should be tried, or punished; it does show that this was an idea that he was prepared to entertain seriously. Others, however, derived a very different message from the second civil war. Many in Parliament were far from enthusiastic about the war that the army was fighting in its name. On 28 April the Commons effectively suspended the Vote of No Addresses and resolved by a large majority that they would not alter the government by king, Lords and Commons. A month later, in response to a request from the City, the Commons agreed to resume negotiations with the king, once religion and the militia had been settled. In June the proceedings against the eleven members were dropped. In July the Commons agreed to negotiate with the king without preconditions: they sought an agreement with the king as part of a wider settlement, which would include the disbanding of the army and the restoration of the old system of local government. On 21 July the Lords refused to declare that the Scots were enemies and ordered the publication of their manifesto.[12] The London common council on 7 August referred to 'our brethren of Scotland'; the Commons replied that they were 'enemies, traitors and rebels'.[13] The day after the Commons received news of the victory at Preston, both Houses agreed to repeal the Vote of No Addresses (suspended earlier), opening the way to resuming negotiations with the king.[14]

The revived intransigence of the Commons was typified by Holles, expelled as one of the eleven members, who now returned. His hatred of the army was undiminished. As a result of the war, he said, 'the meanest of men, the basest and vilest of the nation ... have got the power into their hands, trampled upon the crown, baffled and misused the Parliament, violated the laws, destroyed or suppressed the nobility and gentry'.[15] The House voted to implement the long-delayed Presbyterian church settlement and began to draw up proposals to put to the king. This defiance was probably born of desperation: there was no prospect of anybody being able to challenge the New Model militarily, so the Commons hoped that the king would be equally desperate and would accept their terms with a minimum of quibbling. If he did, and especially if he returned to London, the army might be unable to withstand the huge surge of popular opinion in his favour. It was a high-risk strategy. Quibbling was a central feature of Charles's character, and he still believed that no settlement could be reached without him and so that he was in a strong bargaining position. Privately he made it clear that he had no intention of complying with Parliament's terms: yet again he was negotiating in bad faith.[16] It also rested on the assumption that the army, in the last analysis, would hold back from using blatant military force against Parliament; the march on London in August 1647 could be seen as a move to restore the freedom of Parliament and law and order in London after the riots. It was a dangerous assumption. The army had, after all, used its military might to cow the Presbyterians in Parliament and the City in August 1647, and later in that year there had been repeated calls for it to do so again. After Preston, the army felt isolated and under-valued. There were suspicions that it was being starved of money by Parliament in order to force it to take free quarter, and so further alienate civilians. It reacted angrily to the murder of Rainsborough by a band of Royalists in Yorkshire. Above all, its victory in the second civil war reinforced its conviction that it was right, that God had again witnessed against the king. Discontent festered within the army; anonymous pamphlets viciously attacked the king and called for justice against those responsible for the second civil war, although almost none actually called for the king's execution.[17] There were more than thirty petitions from regiments and garrisons in support of a major Leveller petition to the Commons on 11 September.

The revival of the Levellers owed much to their ability to articulate and publicize the sense of anger and frustration that was widespread inside and outside the army. After two civil wars Parliament had failed to deliver on its promises to secure the liberties of the people. Instead, the same old members were still in place, seemingly impervious to the wishes and rights of the people. No settlement had been achieved, nothing had been done to curb the king. The petition of 11 September was scathing about Parliament's resuming negotiations with the king: he could not be trusted to abide by any promises he made, and would later claim that they had been made under duress. It also asked why the Commons had not proclaimed their superiority over the king and Lords: they represented the people, the source of all legitimate authority, while the king and Lords represented only themselves. It was illogical to have three 'supreme' powers in a state: king, Lords and Commons; only one could be supreme and that had to be the Commons. Though there was no mention of electoral reform or the franchise, the petition went on to demand that the Commons should be made truly accountable to the people, by providing for annual elections. There was a motley collection of other demands, ranging from abolition of tithes to the end of imprisonment for debt and measures to discourage begging. Whereas for much of 1647 the Levellers had denounced the army in general and the grandees in particular as tyrannous and oppressive, the petition now showed at least some concern for the soldiers' interests, calling for constant pay and an indemnity. But it also still called for equality before the law, whereas the indemnity committee privileged soldiers against civilians, and demanded drastic reductions in the level of taxation, which would have made it impossible to pay the army. The petition asked that the power of the king and the House of Lords should be clearly defined, which implied that, despite the hostility expressed towards them in the preamble, the monarchy and Lords would continue. It also called for the abolition of committees and to convey 'all businesses into the true method of the usual trials of the commonwealth', which would militate against putting the king on trial. On the other hand it called for 'justice upon the capital authors and promoters of the former or late wars'.[18]

The petition of 11 September marked the return of the Levellers to somewhere close to the centre of the political stage. It also showed that they were once more seeking to win support within the army, and the response to the petition within the army showed that they were succeeding. Petitions to Fairfax urged the high command to oppose negotiations with the king and adopt the Leveller programme. The soldiers complained bitterly of their arrears and of being forced to take free quarter: they had been paid regularly in the first half of the year but since then they had received little or nothing.[19] Increasingly the Levellers were seen as the voice of the London radicals, and as such a force to be reckoned with; at the very least, they offered a counterweight to the London Presbyterians, who vigorously supported the renewed negotiations with the king. One indication of their perceived importance was that Ireton, their most outspoken adversary at Putney, now sought their support. Completely disillusioned with the king, he now favoured a firm line against both king and Parliament, a view which had relatively few supporters on the army council. His willingness to appeal to the Levellers enhanced their standing, and their dialogue with the army helped give breadth and direction to the growing anger with the king.

The Commons effectively ignored the petition of 11 September; a week later they resumed negotiations with the king, with a set of proposals that were put to him at Newport, Isle of Wight. For the moment there was no reaction from the army, which was busy mopping up pockets of Royalist resistance. On 10 November Ireton put a draft remonstrance before the council of officers, which called for a purge of Parliament and the trial of the king. Fairfax strongly opposed the proposals and the council agreed (with only six votes against) to acquiesce in the outcome of Parliament's negotiations with the king. On the 15th the council of officers agreed to put a final set of proposals to him; these would have left him as little more than a figurehead, and also included provision for regular parliamentary elections and the redistribution of seats. They were probably intended as a sop to those on the army council who still wanted to negotiate with the king, and to give him one last chance to come to terms. They were approved on the 16th (and, predictably, rejected).[20] Ireton's stance won more support from among the rank and file, whose petitions and pressure began to affect the council. Equally significant was a resolution in the Commons on 15 November that the king should be restored to a position of honour and lawful power and allowed to come to London. If the king returned to London there seemed a real possibility of a huge surge of popular support for him that would sweep away all that the army had fought for. On 16 November, the day the army council agreed the final proposals to put to the king, it resolved to present Ireton's remonstrance to Parliament. It accepted a proposal from Lilburne to set up a small committee representing the army, the Levellers, the London Independents and Independent MPs (although only one MP turned up) to recast the remonstrance in a form that was also acceptable to the Levellers. There were only two significant areas of disagreement. The Levellers believed that liberty of conscience should be allowed to all, including Catholics; the army did not. And the Levellers argued that Parliament had no power to punish anyone for offences which were not offences under existing law; the army representatives, who wanted (at the least) to keep open the possibility of putting the king on trial, did not agree.

That said, the areas of agreement in the final version of the remonstrance were far larger than the areas of disagreement. It was presented to the Commons on 20 November; they resolved to lay it aside for a week. It was a massive document, some 25,000 words, and took four hours to read. It reminded Parliament of its Vote of No Addresses and the judgement of

God against the Royalists. It called for a new political system, based on a 'supreme council or Parliament' with the power to make war, pass laws and call offenders to account, even if they had broken no existing law. This political system should be based on the Agreement of the People. Seats in Parliament should be distributed according to population and elections should take place every one or two years. The franchise should be confined to those who subscribed to the Agreement: the traditional property qualification was to be replaced, in effect, by a political one. The thinking behind this was clear: since Putney it had dawned on both the army and the Levellers that free and fair elections might very well lead to the full restoration of the monarchy. The remonstrance catalogued the king's misdeeds. He had broken his 'covenant' to protect the people's liberties (which presumably meant his coronation oath), absolving them from their allegiance. His guilt in the shedding of innocent blood had to be expiated. There was no point in negotiating with him as he would not be bound by the most solemn agreements; his popularity, which was acknowledged, was an additional reason not to negotiate. The remonstrance therefore called for an end to negotiations and the trial and condemnation of the king.[21]

The remonstrance was the most trenchant statement yet of the case against the king, although it should be noted that it did not call for the king's execution, or the abolition of the monarchy; indeed, it implied that the monarchy would continue, in a much weakened form, with the king as a figurehead. The Commons' cool response to the remonstrance, and determination to continue negotiating with the king, can have come as little surprise to either the army or the Levellers. Fairfax, realizing the strength of feeling in the army, now sent a stern message to the Commons that the army was coming to London to achieve the ends set out in the remonstrance, and sent orders to secure the king's person. Charles was moved from Carisbrooke to Hurst Castle, where he was kept in close confinement. The army's headquarters were moved from St

Alban's to Windsor where, in an eight-hour prayer meeting, it was resolved to quarter troops in and around the City. The army arrived soon after and a substantial part took up quarters in the City; eventually, as the City still failed to pay its arrears of taxation, a troop of cavalry was quartered in St Paul's Cathedral, a deliberate affront to both the citizens' civic pride and the sensibilities of adherents of the national Church. Presbyterian and Royalist 'conspirators' were rounded up, and Fairfax announced that the army would remain in the City until all the arrears of the monthly assessment had been paid. There were clashes between soldiers and civilians and some looting: the soldiers clearly felt that the City deserved to be punished.

The high command had no clear idea what to do with Parliament. They may have hoped that, as in July 1647 the House of Commons might purge itself of 'corrupt' members. When it showed no sign of doing so, Ireton wanted to dissolve it, but others argued that this would create more problems than it solved. If the army got rid of this Parliament it would soon need another, to vote taxes and to give at least a façade of legality to the regime. A general election, even on the sort of politically restricted franchise envisaged in the remonstrance, might well produce a House of Commons favourable to the king and deeply hostile to the army. The army's allies in Parliament proposed a purge, similar to that of the eleven members in 1647, but much more extensive. Ireton and his fellow generals were unsure what to do, until their minds were made up by events in the Commons. On 2 December an ordinance returned control of the county militia to the gentry. All through the 4th and into the morning of the 5th the Commons debated the king's response to the propositions of Newport and eventually resolved that it constituted a sufficient basis to proceed to a settlement; the resolution did not say that the response was satisfactory. For one last time the Presbyterian majority in the Commons had defied the army. During the rest of the 5th, the army's allies in the Commons drew up a list of those who had supported the resolution and those who, in

August, had opposed a declaration that the Scots were invaders and rebels. On the morning of 6 December, as members arrived at the House, they found a troop of musketeers guarding the door, commanded by Colonel Thomas Pride, who was said to have been a brewer's drayman before joining the army. Consulting the list prepared the day before, Pride arrested about forty-five members (accounts vary) and prevented over fifty more from taking their seats. Others stayed away in protest. With the committed Presbyterians, and some moderates, gone, the Independents dominated the Commons for the first time since 1646. An order that members should declare their detestation of the vote of 5 December before they could take their seats drove out more. In the end forty-five members were imprisoned and 186 excluded; by 14 December it was difficult to secure a quorum (forty).[22]

The truncated House of Commons, and the handful of peers who remained in the Lords, were regarded by the public with a mixture of indignation and ridicule. They were soon nick-named the Rump, the back end of a Parliament, and boys in London called out 'kiss my Parliament'. Neither the Parliament nor the army had any clear idea how to proceed: the purge had been designed to prevent agreement between Parliament and king, with no programme in mind. The army officers demanded that the eleven members 'impeached' by the army in 1647 should be brought to trial, but many still favoured negotiations with the king: now that he had no hope of a deal with the Presbyterians, he could be expected to be more amenable. At this stage only a smallish minority of officers favoured putting the king on trial. Ireton, conscious of his isolation, plunged into further negotiations with the Levellers about the form of a second Agreement of the People that was be presented to Parliament. On the former points of contention, Ireton got his way. There was to be no freedom of worship for papists or 'prelatists' – strictly speaking, supporters of episcopacy, in practice also those who wished to use the Prayer Book; and Parliament was to have the power to punish where no existing law had been broken. The franchise was now confined to male householders, assessed for the poor rate, who were not servants, wage-earners or (initially) Royalists – and who had subscribed to the Agreement: in other words, a form of property qualification had been added to the political qualification required in the remonstrance. Those who had signed the London engagement of 1647 (calling for negotiations with the king) or petitioned for a truce with the Scots in 1648 were ineligible for election to Parliament. Rather than a call for democracy, here was a blueprint for a dictatorship of the godly.[23]

The Agreement was eventually presented to Parliament in January, and rejected. The army leaders soon forgot about it, but the thinking behind the electoral proposals bore fruit in London. In the common council elections at the end of December all those who had subscribed a petition in favour of negotiating with the king were debarred from voting. More 'malignants' were weeded out on various pretexts early in 1649. Now that the City government shared the aims of the army, the obstruction of tax-paying ended. In January the common council petitioned Parliament to take firm action against those who had been responsible for the late war against Parliament. The army had long been aware that it was out of step with civilian opinion and had claimed that the righteousness of the cause mattered more than numbers; indeed, this could be seen as growing out of the Puritan belief that the truly godly were a 'remnant', traduced and reviled by the ungodly majority. It is striking, if sad, that the Levellers had come to think the same way. The provisions in the second Agreement, attempting to confine political rights to the politically 'right', were a far cry from Rainsborough's ringing endorsement of universal manhood suffrage at Putney a little over a year before.

Also during December a last set of proposals were sent to the king by the Derby House peers, via the earl of Denbigh. They included the abolition of the king's negative voice and of episcopacy, and a promise to seek no help from either Scotland or Ireland; they apparently gave no clear indication of the powers that Charles would enjoy if he concurred. One reason for this approach was that the majority even in the purged Parliament, and probably in the army, would have preferred a negotiated settlement to putting the king on trial. Far from being wished for or inevitable, regicide was one of the most unlikely possible outcomes to the convoluted politics of December 1648 and 1649.[24] On the 25th the army council voted overwhelmingly that if he accepted the Denbigh terms his life should be spared.[25] Another reason for this approach to the king was an impending agreement between Ormond and the Confederate Catholics, which raised the prospect that Ormond might soon gain control of all of Ireland and be able to mount an invasion of England; the Confederates also now had a fleet, which opened the prospect of a naval alliance with the Dutch. Confidence, probably exaggerated, that the Irish would come to his rescue led the king to reject what were, in themselves, unattractive terms. Indeed, he refused to admit Denbigh to his presence. The army council responded by ordering that he should no longer be treated with the formalities normally due to a king.[26]

With the door to a negotiated settlement apparently firmly shut, Parliament felt that it had to apply more pressure. On 1 January 1649 the Commons passed a bill to try the king on a charge of treason, for levying war against Parliament and the people. When the Lords rejected this, partly on the grounds that it was far from clear that what he was accused of was treason under existing law, the Commons resolved that, as the sole representative of the people, it exercised supreme power in the kingdom and its resolutions had the force of law without the need for the Lords' concurrence. They then passed an 'Act' (not an ordinance) to set up a high court of justice to try the king.[27] If it was intended that the threat of a trial would browbeat the king into submission, it failed. The move intensified the activities of a variety of interested parties. The Scots, including those most opposed to the Engagement, were outraged that the English were apparently planning to try and even execute their king. Some Royalists tried to save the Royalist cause from the king, whose conduct had made him a liability, suggesting that a regency might be established, as if the king were insane, or else that he should be deposed (or 'abdicate') and one of his sons made king in his place. For the proponents of this plan it was unfortunate that Charles's two older sons were abroad, but the third, Henry, duke of Gloucester, was in Parliament's custody. From the Dutch Republic, the greatest naval power in Europe, came diplomatic pressure not to harm the king: the stadhouder, or chief governor and military commander, William II, prince of Orange, was married to Charles's daughter Mary. All these frenetic negotiations and intrigues added to the general uncertainty about what the trial was intended to achieve, but it seemed most improbable that it would end with the conviction and condign punishment of the king. The hope remained strong that, faced with the prospect of condemnation and death, Charles would at last see sense, admit that he had to some extent been in the wrong, and consent to a viable political settlement.

The court finally convened on 20 January. Westminster Hall was where the public courts of justice sat, and where Strafford's trial had been held. Indeed, there were strong parallels between the two trials, notably the attempts to prove the accused guilty of treason, using legal arguments, when the real 'charge' against him was that he was too dangerous to be allowed to live. The hall was cleared of the booksellers' stalls that were usually there and a stage was built. The royal arms were displayed prominently in the painted chamber and on the mace. Two hundred guards were intended to emphasize the solemnity of what was intended, as in Strafford's case, to be a very public occasion, and to discourage outbursts from spectators; this did not prevent a masked lady (widely known to be Lady Fairfax) loudly denying the legitimacy of the court. The setting, robes and paraphernalia were designed to emphasize the authority and dignity of the court, a body capable of calling even a king to account, in the name of the people. The charge against him was that, although he was 'trusted with a limited power to govern by and according to the laws of the land', he had ruled as 'a tyrant, traitor, murderer and a public and implacable enemy of the commonwealth of England'.[28]

It seems likely that the majority of those sitting in the court expected that Charles would be persuaded to plead guilty to a few specimen charges. He might then be sentenced to a nominal punishment, or perhaps declared deposed – although with his eldest son in Holland that might not have been a sensible move. What nobody apparently considered was what to do if the king refused to plead, which he did repeatedly. As so often, he exaggerated the strength of his position and seemed to regard the trial as an elaborate process of negotiation. Again and again, he stated that he did not recognize the court and asked what authority it had to try him: in his eyes, it could not legally try anyone, least of all a king. 'If power without law may make laws, may alter the fundamental laws of the kingdom, I do not know what subject he is in England that can be sure of his life, or anything that he calls his own.'[29] After the Commons' vote that they were the supreme power in the land, and all the efforts that had been made to emphasize the authority and majesty of the court, the judges could not ignore the king's defiance. Some, however, were discomfited by the king's arguments. Only 68 of the 135 judges named by the Commons appeared on 20 January. Some already had reservations about sitting and soon began to stay away from the court. As the king continued to deny the legality of the court, to the anger of the soldiers, the doughty Lady Fairfax denied that the Rump represented the people, and spectators cried 'God save the king'. The judges disagreed over what to do next. While on 24 and 25 January the court heard evidence to show that the king had made actual war against his people, leading armies into battle and bringing in foreign forces, the key issue was no longer the king's guilt but whether he was to be punished for refusing to accept the authority of the court. Under the common law, the punishment for refusing to plead was death, and the prospect that the king might be sentenced to death raised the lobbying and intrigues to a new level. The Scottish Parliament sent a protest, and an embassy arrived hotfoot from Holland. Even after the court had agreed on a death sentence, Charles was given more chances to plead and so recognize the authority of the court. Some of the judges were prepared to give him even more time, but their colleagues had had enough, and on the 26th the court resolved that he was guilty on the charge of being a 'tyrant, traitor and murderer' and was to be beheaded. The king was not allowed to respond to the closing speech of the president of the court and was dragged from the court crying, 'I am not suffered to speak.'[30] Soldiers blew smoke and gunpowder in his face. The death warrant was signed by fifty-nine members of the court, of whom eighteen were army officers, including Cromwell and Ireton.

Even in 1647 there had been those who believed that the king should be tried and possibly executed; at the end of 1648 these were probably a smallish minority in the army and were certainly a small minority in the nation at large. The trial marked the final stage in a long chain of events which started with Charles's refusal to accept what everyone else, except perhaps his wife, saw as the logical consequence of his defeat in the civil war: that he would have to make concessions and become a different sort of king. His refusal to make concessions can be explained partly by a conviction that something was bound to turn up that would enable him to recover all the powers of the monarchy – if not from England, then perhaps from Scotland, or Ireland, or Holland. There was also a stubborn core of principle within his deviousness, the belief that the powers of the monarchy, or the episcopal government of the Church of England, were not his to give away. But there was another deeper element too – he was not going to be swayed by the fear of death. In general, he showed neither guilt nor remorse for his conduct, though there was one striking exception: he could not forgive himself for sacrificing

Strafford, just as he could never forgive those responsible for Strafford's death. For this weakness, this sin, he deserved divine punishment and, especially in times of trouble, he seemed to regard this prospect almost with equanimity. As early as 1642 he told Hamilton 'I have set my rest on the justice of my cause, being resolved that no extremity or misfortune shall make me yield. For either I will be a glorious king or a patient martyr.'[31] For those who saw Charles as incorrigibly devious, these remarks would have been incomprehensible, but they show that no amount of pressure could make him yield when he was determined not to do so. Those who organized and took part in the trial had not expected or wished to make him a martyr, but in effect they did so.

The final act in the tragedy came on 30 January. Charles was taken to the Banqueting House, in Whitehall, designed by Inigo Jones to emphasize the dignity of monarchy; the ceiling, by Rubens, showed James I ascending into heaven. The king wore two shirts: it was a cold morning, and he did not want to shiver and to seem afraid. A vast crowd stood silently around the black, draped scaffold. As with every person facing execution, he was allowed to say a few words, but the rows of soldiers around the scaffold made it very difficult for the people to hear him. He prayed briefly, and then told those of the crowd who could hear him that he was going from a corruptible to an incorruptible crown. He desired the liberty of the people as much as any, but liberty 'consists in having government, those laws by which their lives and their goods may be most their own. It is not their having a share in the government; that is nothing appertaining unto them. A subject and a sovereign are clean different things.'[32] He appeared calm and, as during his trial, it was alleged that there was no sign of his habitual stammer. Then he laid down his head and the masked executioner struck it from his body with a single blow. The soldiers guarding the scaffold cheered; the crowd groaned.

EPILOGUE

Pride's Purge and the king's execution marked the triumph of the army and its few civilian allies. That triumph was crowned by the abolition of the monarchy and the House of Lords: so few peers now attended that there could be no pretence that they formed a meaningful 'House'. England was declared a 'Commonwealth' or 'free state'. A new great seal, without the royal arms, had been ordered before the king's trial: it bore the legend 'in the first year of freedom, by God's blessing restored'.[1] The new regime was in some ways to live up to the confidence expressed in this motto. By 1652 the New Model had completely conquered both Scotland and Ireland, something no monarch had ever managed to achieve. In the next few years a much enlarged navy was able to take on the greatest naval power in Europe, the Dutch Republic, and to emerge with honour, if not with total victory. After a naval expedition to the Caribbean, in some ways badly mismanaged, England emerged with Jamaica. Soon after, the New Model joined with the French against Spain in Flanders and gained Dunkirk, the first English possession on the Continent since the loss of Calais a century before. These military and naval successes were in stark contrast to the dismal performance of Charles I's government at Cadiz and La Rochelle in the 1620s. For the first time since the reign of Henry VIII England was a major military force in Europe and the nation's prestige and self-confidence grew accordingly. Meanwhile, the Navigation Act of 1651 attempted to secure for the English a monopoly of trade with England's colonies and an opportunity to muscle in on the international carrying trade, dominated by the Dutch; the much enlarged navy made it possible to enforce the terms of the Act. The foundations of the massive increase in colonial and overseas trade after 1660 were laid in the 1650s.

The military successes of the regime contrasted starkly with its political weakness. The army remained self-consciously untypical of English opinion. It had carried through Pride's Purge and the regicide, which had been deplored not only by Royalists but the great majority of Parliamentarians. Even among those who sat in the Rump, only a minority whole-heartedly supported the army and shared its commitment to godly reform. Many members of the council of state, the new executive body set up by the Rump, failed to take the Engagement, a declaration of fidelity to the new regime, without a king or House of Lords. But if few fully accepted the legitimacy of the new regime, its military successes won at least grudging admiration. The punishment of those 'guilty' of complicity in the 1641 Irish rising met with general approval: they were either deported or lost their land and the power of the Catholic landowners was broken. The English had few complaints, either, about the humbling of an increasingly rigid and intolerant Covenanter regime in Scotland. On a day-to-day level, government continued to function. County government gradually returned to the old ways; the county committees were wound up, and power returned to the justices of the peace. Moderate Parliamentarians and even the sons of Royalists (including the Protestant grandson of the earl of

Worcester) were appointed as magistrates. The law courts functioned almost normally too, so interpersonal disputes could be resolved peacefully in the usual way.

And yet there were limits to the return to normality. There was instability at the top. The relationship between the Rump and the army was always fraught. They were yoked together by the need to preserve the republic, and the Rump made heroic efforts to provide the funds that paid for the army's military successes. But the majority of the Rump had few ambitions beyond survival, whereas the army was zealous for godly reform. It called for sweeping legal reforms, to make the law simpler and more accessible to the layman. It demanded religious reform, including the abolition of tithes, which supported the parish clergy, but in many cases were collected by wealthy laymen. The army's reform programme thus threatened the interests of three powerful vested interests: the lawyers, the clergy and the gentry. Finally, the army called for an end to the present Parliament and fresh elections. Its leaders had long since abandoned the ideal of universal manhood suffrage: few had probably held it in the first place. Like the Levellers, the army accepted the need to ensure that the right to vote was exercised only by those politically and morally fit to use it, and that there should be provisions to ensure that those who sat in Parliament were godly and of good character. The populace, as a whole, could not be trusted to choose the right people. As one republican put it in 1655, 'I am for trusting the people with their liberties as soon as any, but when . . . the major part grow corrupt they must be regulated.'[2] Perhaps the most fundamental point at issue between the Rump and the army was the mechanism for ensuring that future Parliaments consisted of godly members. This was the issue that led to Cromwell's forcible dissolution of the Rump in April 1653. After an experiment with a nominated Parliament of supposedly godly men, in December the army adopted a new constitution, the Instrument of Government, which established Cromwell as Lord Protector. From then on,

Cromwell edged slowly back towards something more like the old regime. There was now a single-person executive and an elected Parliament, albeit one chosen on a narrower franchise, especially in the counties. In 1657, although Cromwell refused the crown, the Protectorate was made hereditary and a second chamber, or Other House, was established. In 1659, under Oliver's successor, Richard, the old parliamentary constituencies and franchise were restored. Together with the return to relative normality in county government, the regime resembled more and more the one that had existed before the civil war.

But the resemblance went only so far. Cromwell was only too aware of the potential threat from Royalist plotting, and the concern for security led to a curtailing of individual liberty. This was most apparent in the aftermath of a relatively ineffectual Royalist rising in 1655. The government imposed a new tax on Royalists, whether or not there was any evidence that they had been implicated in the rising, and made them enter into stringent bonds to be of good behaviour; their movements were monitored and if they came to London they had to register with the authorities. The Protectorate was always eager to impose godly behaviour, and in 1655–6 the country was placed under the rule of eleven major-generals, whose task was to stir local magistrates to suppress ungodly behaviour and, in particular, to prevent gatherings (like race meetings or cock fights) which could serve as a cover for Royalist plotting. Apart from the restrictions on Royalists, it is doubtful whether these measures were particularly successful, but (together with a harsh response to legal challenges to some forms of taxation) they showed the authoritarian reality behind the apparent return to normality and legality.

There can be no doubt the further the Protectorate moved back towards the old regime, the more support, or acquiescence, it would win. Moderate Parliamentarians and Royalists wanted to get rid of the army, to re-establish a national church (with no toleration for sectaries) and to bring back the monarchy. Cromwell could not deliver on any of these. For him, the great gain of the civil wars was religious liberty. He was prepared to maintain a national church, in the sense of a public provision of worship in the parishes, paid for by tithes. But he insisted that the government should ensure that the parish clergy were educationally and morally suitable and that those who wished to opt out of parish worship should be free to do so. This religious liberty could survive only while England remained a republic and that, in turn, depended on the army. Cromwell made great efforts to ensure that England did not become a military dictatorship, but he was prepared to act dictatorially if the safety of the regime required it, and he was in no doubt that in the final analysis his power depended on the army. He thus had to strike a delicate balance, moving back towards the old order to win the allegiance of the civilian population without upsetting the army, which remained wedded to ideals of godly reform. Only Oliver, with his credentials as both a soldier and an MP, could do this; his son, Richard, lacked the respect and trust of the army and his rule collapsed within a year. The need for the army's support limited how far Oliver could return to the old order; fear of alienating the army was one reason for his refusing the crown in 1657.

After Oliver's death, and Richard's fall from power, it became hard to hide the naked fact of army rule. It was significant that the army felt the need for a Parliament after Richard's fall, to give a civilian façade to the government and to provide a body that could vote taxes. As it could not trust the electorate to choose a suitable Parliament, the army leaders reinstated the Rump. The relationship soon broke down again, and the army expelled the Rump, but now the army was itself divided. The commander-in-chief in Scotland, General Monk, demanded that the Rump, from which he derived his authority, should be restored. There was growing resistance to the army's authority. Supporters of the Rump seized Portsmouth and Dublin, part of the fleet blockaded the Thames, the judges refused to try any cases and there was a widespread refusal to pay taxes. Soldiers in London, jeered and spat at wherever they went, became demoralized and confused, uncertain who or what they were supposed to be fighting for. On 26 December the Rump reconvened; the commander-in-chief of the army in England declared that God had spat in his face.

The events of the last months of 1659 showed that the people of England would not tolerate naked military rule. The next few months were to show that, encouraged (as in 1640) by the prospect of deliverance from Scotland – Monk's army entered England on 1 January 1660 – they did not want the Rump or the republic either. As Monk marched south, he was inundated with petitions calling for a free Parliament, which would restore the nation's liberties and (although almost no one mentioned it) the monarchy. Monk was sufficiently impressed by the overwhelming tide of public opinion that in February he ordered the Rump to readmit the surviving 'secluded members' – those who had been expelled, or who had withdrawn, at Pride's Purge. This restored the Commons as it had been in December 1648, with a majority in favour of a settlement with the king and an ordered national church. The Commons did their utmost, before dissolving themselves in March, to ensure that the next general election (to be held in April) produced an overwhelmingly Parliamentarian body, which could ensure that the monarchy was restored under the sort of restrictions envisaged in the propositions of Newport in 1648. But the electorate had other ideas and the Convention that assembled in April was fairly evenly divided between men of Parliamentarian and Royalist backgrounds; 'qualifications' prescribed by Parliament were widely ignored. It quickly resolved to proclaim the king and to invite him to return. The Royalists were strong enough to prevent any preconditions being imposed on him, so he returned without any formal restrictions on his powers. The precise terms of his restoration would be negotiated, or simply emerge, after his return.

Charles II's return to England owed little to Royalist plotting (which had generally been small scale or inept) or to his own efforts. His attempts to win the assistance of the Dutch, French and Spanish governments had been spectacularly unsuccessful. The one positive contribution he made to his restoration was in his Declaration of Breda in April 1660. In this he reassured those who had sided with Parliament that his return would pose no threat to their personal safety or property. In particular, he promised to agree to a general bill of indemnity, in which Parliament would decide who was to be excluded from pardon. (In the event, this meant mostly those who had signed the king's death warrant.) What was not in doubt was the enormous popular enthusiasm for the return of the monarchy. This was seen in the celebrations following the proclamation of the king and his progress to London, which he entered on 29 May, his thirtieth birthday: the road was lined with cheering crowds all the way from Rochester to London. This enthusiasm reflected not only relief at a return to traditional ordered government, free from the rule of the meddlesome and self-righteous godly few. It was also an expression of something much deeper, a veneration for the mystical and divine attributes of monarchy, passed on by blood from one monarch to another and recognized in the ceremony of anointing at the coronation. One aspect of these attributes was the belief that the king could cure scrofula by his royal touch. This belief was held not only by ignorant peasants and credulous Anglicans, but by the hard-headed aldermen of the traditionally Puritan cities of Norwich and Bristol, who granted money to pay for those suffering from scrofula to go to be touched by the king. Charles II touched thousands for the king's evil in the course of his reign and, cynic though he was in many ways, he took the ceremony of touching very seriously, knowing how important it was to maintain a public image of divinity and dignity. In his later years, he would hold it in St George's Chapel at Windsor, in front of a large mural depicting Christ healing the sick. He was also careful to maintain an appropriate degree of ceremony at court, to maintain the image of the monarch as being at once remote and accessible.[3]

It might seem that Charles's efforts to refurbish the aura of monarchy marked a conscious attempt to undo the damage done by his father's execution. Nothing would be further from the truth. As even his closest supporters were aware, Charles I had been a disastrous king, whose deviousness and incompetence had done the monarchy great harm. All this was undone by the manner of his death. In his trial he posed (for pose it surely was) as a sacrificial victim, taking it upon himself to die for the sake of his people at the hands of an illegitimate authority. The parallels with Christ were obvious and were developed explicitly in *Eikon Basilike*, which first appeared in print only ten days after his execution. This volume, supposedly a collection of his prison writings, must have been in preparation even before his trial and became one of the publishing successes of the century. Its frontispiece showed the king kneeling, his earthly crown on the ground, a crown of thorns in his hand, and his eyes looking up to where a heavenly crown awaited him. Lest his death be forgotten, an Act of Parliament of 1661 ordered an annual day of fasting and humiliation on 30 January, which provided an opportunity for parsons to wax lyrical on the wickedness of regicide and the sinfulness of resistance to royal authority A deep revulsion at his execution, and anger against those who had 'murdered' him, provided such strong emotional support for the restored monarchy that for decades hardly anyone could be found to defend the regicide, or to criticize the late king.

The revulsion against regicide helps explain why the monarchy – and for a while the House of Stuart – survived the civil wars. It was an act supported and defended by very few. The English were a law abiding and governable people, and in the 1640s the momentum of events had led them into areas which they had not sought and which they profoundly disliked. On the other hand, their acceptance of authority was linked to expectations about how that authority should be exercised and these certainly did not go away at the Restoration. Indeed, the explosion of news and of public knowledge of government and politics in the 1640s meant that those expectations were enhanced and more widely disseminated through the population. Never before had English men and women received so much information about public affairs and discussed them so extensively. Charles II accepted, as James I and Charles I had not, the need to get the views of his government across to his people. Thanks to the bitter experience of the civil wars, very many of them were prepared to listen. Despite his instinct for avoiding trouble, Charles sometimes provoked suspicion and resentment, but the fundamental conservatism of a large proportion of the population, and bitter memories of the civil wars, helped to ensure that he survived. At the same time, the partisan politics of the last part of his reign ensured that the divisions of Whig and Tory, which in some ways replicated those of the civil wars, continued into the eighteenth century and beyond. In the reign of queen Anne newspapers fiercely debated the rights and wrongs of the civil wars and well into the eighteenth century Tory crowds on election days chanted slogans referring to the 1640s and 1650s. For better or worse, the experience of civil war had left its mark on the national psyche.

NOTES

Chapter 1

1   Clarendon, i.93.
2   A. Fletcher, 'The Coming of War', in Morrill, *Reactions*, 36.
3   D. Hirst, 'The English Republic and the Making of Britain', in B. Bradshaw and J.S. Morrill (eds), *The British Problem c. 1534–1707* (Basingstoke, 1996), 198.
4   See N. Canny, *Making Ireland British, 1580–1650* (Oxford, 2001).
5   S. Hindle, 'Hierarchy and Community in the Elizabethan Parish: The Swallowfield Articles of 1596', *HJ*, 42 (1999), 835–51.

Chapter 2

1   P. Collinson, *The Religion of Protestants: The Church in English Society 1559–1625* (Oxford, 1982), 144–5.
2   D. Cressy, *England on Edge: Crisis and Revolution 1640–2* (Oxford, 2006), ch. 4.

Chapter 3

1   Gardiner, *History*, ix.288.
2   A. Fletcher, *The Outbreak of the English Civil War* (London, 1981), 111.

3   Cressy, *England on Edge*, 97–101.
4   See C. Hibbard, *Charles I and the Popish Plot* (Chapel Hill, 1983).
5   J. Adamson, *The Noble Revolt: The Overthrow of Charles I* (London, 2007), 44–52.
6   Gardiner, *History*, ix.229.
7   Ibid., ix.336.
8   Ibid., ix.246–7.
9   Fletcher, *Outbreak*, 35–40.
10 C. Russell, 'The First Army Plot of 1641', *TRHS*, 5th series, 38 (1988), 95–6 and *passim*; Adamson, *Revolt*, 279–84.
11 Russell, 'Army Plot', 100–1.
12 C. Russell, *The Fall of the British Monarchies, 1637–42* (Oxford, 1991), 211, 285.
13 Ibid., 275.
14 Gardiner, *History*, ix.340.
15 Adamson, *Revolt*, 265–6, 270, 272 (quoted).
16 Kenyon, 200–1; Adamson, *Revolt*, 290.
17 Fletcher, *Outbreak*, 79.
18 Gardiner, *History*, ix.355.
19 Fletcher, *Outbreak*, 31–2.
20 Gardiner, *History*, ix.367.
21 Ibid., ix.341.
22 Ibid., ix.375–6. The news was leaked by Lady Carlisle.
23 Fletcher, *Outbreak*, 55–9.
24 Gardiner, *History*, ix.400–2.
25 Fletcher, *Outbreak*, 102–7.
26 Adamson, *Revolt*, 329–31, 342–3.
27 Gardiner, *History*, ix.298.
28 Fletcher, *Outbreak*, 117.
29 Lindley, 64.
30 Gardiner, *History*, ix.285.
31 See C. Hill, 'The Many-headed Monster', in C. Hill, *Change and Continuity in Seventeenth-century England* (London, 1974), ch. 8.
32 Lindley, 64.
33 J. Walter, *Understanding Popular Violence in the English Revolution: The Colchester Plunderers* (Cambridge, 1999).
34 Lindley, 94–5.
35 Fletcher, *Outbreak*, 76–7.

Chapter 4

1   See Canny, *Making Ireland British*, ch. 8.
2   Gardiner, *Documents*, 206–7.
3   Ibid., 229.
4   Ibid., 231–2.
5   Ibid., 203.
6   Cressy, *England on Edge*, 383–4.
7   Gardiner, *Documents*, pp. 236–7.
8   The details are obscure: see Russell, *Fall*, 432 (and n. 141), 449; V. Pearl, *London and the Outbreak of the Puritan Revolution* (Oxford, 1961), 139–41.
9   Gardiner, *History*, x.162–3.
10 Fletcher, *Outbreak*, 293.
11 Ibid., 186.
12 Ibid., 288.
13 History of Parliament, 1640–60 Section, unpublished entry on Shrewsbury, by Stephen Roberts.
14 Gardiner, *History*, x.196.
15 Gardiner, *Documents*, 249–54 (quote from 254).
16 Kenyon, 18–20 (quote from 20).
17 Cressy, *England on Edge*, 219.
18 Fletcher, *Outbreak*, 379.
19 G.E. Aylmer, *The King's Servants: The Civil Service of Charles I* (London, 1961), 381–2. For Rudyerd's somewhat mixed record, see Morrill, *Revolt (2)*, 31–2.
20 Fletcher, *Outbreak*, 414.
21 Morrill, *Revolt (2)*, 62. See also C. Carlton, *Going to the Wars: The Experience of the British Civil Wars, 1638–51* (London, 1992), 291.
22 R. Hutton, *The Royalist War Effort, 1642–6* (London, 1982), 11–12, 24–5.
23 Gardiner, *History*, x.206.
24 Clarendon, ii.291.

Chapter 5

1   M. Stoyle, 'English "Nationalism", Celtic Particularism and the English Civil War', *HJ*, 43 (2000), 1113–28.
2   Hutton, *War Effort*, 14.
3   D. Underdown, *Pride's Purge: Politics in the English Revolution* (Oxford, 1971), 59, 63.
4   Kenyon, 240.

5   For a fuller account of the county committees, see the next chapter.
6   Warwick, so influential in 1640–2, became a marginal political figure, although he remained as lord admiral until 1648.
7   Gardiner, *GCW*, i.303–7; Morrill, *Revolt (2)*, 84.
8   Morrill, *Revolt (2)*, 92–3.
9   Ibid., 75.
10 Gardiner, *GCW*, ii.181.
11 Ibid., ii.59.
12 I. Gentles, 'The Choosing of Officers in the New Model Army', *Historical Research*, 67 (1994), 264–85.
13 I. Roots (ed.), *Speeches of Oliver Cromwell* (London, 1989), 134.
14 I. Gentles, *The New Model Army in England, Scotland and Ireland, 1645–53* (Oxford, 1992), 105.
15 D. Scott, 'The "Northern Gentlemen", the Parliamentary Independents and Anglo-Scottish Relations in the Long Parliament', *HJ*, 42 (1999), 347–75.
16 Gardiner, *GCW*, iii.5, 33–4, 40–2, 69–71.
17 Ibid., ii.287.
18 Ibid., ii.317, 374–6, iii.19.
19 See R. Ashton, 'From Cavalier to Roundhead Tyranny', in Morrill, *Reactions*, ch. 8.

Chapter 6

1   Morrill, *Revolt (1)*, 184–5.
2   D. Pennington, 'The War and the People', in Morrill, *Reactions*, 132–3.
3   Morrill, *Revolt (1)*, 181.
4   Ibid., 205.
5   Morrill, *Revolt (2)*, 194.
6   M. Braddick, *Parliamentary Taxation in Seventeenth Century England* (Woodbridge, 1994), 274.
7   Morrill, *Revolt (2)*, 118.
8   Carlton, *Going to the Wars*, 94.
9   Morrill, *Revolt (2)*, 120–2; Morrill, *Revolt (1)*, 173–4.
10 Morrill, *Revolt (1)*, 178–9.
11 P. Tennant, 'Parish and People: South Warwickshire in the English Civil War', in R.C. Richardson (ed.), *The English Civil War: Local Aspects* (Stroud, 1997), 177.
12 Carlton, *Going to the Wars*, 282.
13 Hutton, *Royalist War Effort*, 43.

14   I. Roy, 'England Turned Germany? The Aftermath of the Civil War in its European Context', *TRHS*, 5th Series, 28 (1978) 136n.

15   I. Roy, 'The English Civil War and English Society', in *War and Society*, 37–8.

16   Carlton, *Going to the Wars*, 253–4.

17   Underdown, *Pride's Purge*, 78

18   Thomson, 118.

19   Roy, 'England Turned Germany', 136–7.

20   Carlton, *Going to the Wars*, 273.

21   M. Stoyle (ed.), '"Whole Streets Converted to Ashes": Property Destruction in Exeter during the English Civil War', in Richardson, *English Civil War*, 129–44.

22   Carlton, *Going to the Wars*, ch. 9, summary p. 214.

23   Ibid., 173, 257–8. (The second reference gives different figures to the first.)

24   B. Donagan, 'Codes and Conduct in the English Civil War', *P & P*, 118 (1988), 74–82. M. Ó Siochrú, 'Atrocity, Codes of Conduct and the Irish in the British Civil Wars, 1641–53', *P & P*, 195 (2007), 55–86, argues plausibly that the arrival of professionals reduced the level of atrocities in Ireland.

25   Gardiner, *GCW*, ii.363–5.

26   Gentles, *New Model*, 131.

27   Ó Siochrú, 'Atrocity', 68–70. This states that those killed after Naseby were Welsh; Ian Roy assures me that they were Irish.

28   Thomson, 152–60.

29   Morrill, *Revolt (1)*, 190–2.

30   C. Holmes, *The Eastern Association in the English Civil War* (Cambridge, 1974), 63–5.

31   Morrill, *Revolt (1)*, 195.

32   Donagan, 'Codes and Conduct', 89–95; Carlton, *Going to the Wars*, 243–4.

33   Morrill, 'The Church in England, 1642–9', in Morrill, *Reactions*, 93, 107–8. My obligations to this groundbreaking essay are obvious. See also R. Ashton, *Counter-Revolution: The Second Civil War and its Origins 1646–8* (New Haven, 1994), ch. 7.

34   See the case of Edward Jude, Thomson, 199–204. More generally, see I. Green, 'The Persecution of "Scandalous" and "Malignant" Clergy during the English Civil War', *English Historical Review*, 94 (1979), 507–31.

35 A. Hopper, 'Fitted for Desperation: Honour and Treachery in Parliament's Yorkshire Command, 1642–3', *History*, 86 (2001), 140–2.
36 Morrill, *Revolt (2)*, 136.
37 Lindley, 134.
38 Hutton, *Royalist War Effort*, 158–65, 170–1.
39 Roy, 'Civil War and English Society', in *War and Society*, 39–42.
40 Hutton, *Royalist War Effort*, 183–6.
41 See the forthright petition of the Sussex Clubmen in September 1645: Morrill, *Revolt (1)*, 198–9.

Chapter 7

1 Ashton, *Counter-Revolution*, ch. 2 (entitled, appropriately, 'No Peace Dividend').
2 Ibid., 205–9.
3 Woodhouse, 388.
4 Gardiner, *GCW*, iii.72.
5 Ibid., iii.135–6.
6 A. Woolrych, *Soldiers and Statesmen: The General Council of the Army, 1647–8* (Oxford, 1987), 177.
7 V. Pearl, 'London's Counter-Revolution', in G.E. Aylmer (ed.), *The Interregnum* (London, 1972), ch. 1.
8 Gardiner, *GCW*, iii.215.
9 See G. Catemario, 'The Political Making of the New Model Army, 1644–7' (unpublished PhD thesis, London, 2002).
10 Woolrych, *Soldiers*, 38; Gentles, *New Model*, 149–51.
11 B. Donagan, 'The Army, the State and the Soldier in the English Civil War', in Mendle, 91–2; Gentles, *New Model*, 121–5. Only a small minority of indemnity cases relating to soldiers involved those of the New Model: ibid., 129.
12 Woolrych, *Soldiers*, 36–7.
13 Donagan, 'Army, State and Soldier', in Mendle, 92–5.
14 Carlton, *Going to the Wars*, 183.
15 Woodhouse, 396–8.
16 Ibid., 399.
17 Phil Baker, who has worked extensively on the early Levellers, argues that the term 'Leveller' was not used until 1648 and that those now labelled 'Levellers' by historians formed a small part of the wider body of radical Independents (or 'well affected') of London. However, as the term is widely used by historians when dealing with 1647, I shall use it too.

18 I. Gentles, 'Arrears of Pay and Ideology in the Army Revolt of 1647', in *War and Society*, 49–50; Woodhouse, 398–9.
19 Gentles, *New Model*, 159, 168.
20 Gardiner, *GCW*, iii.262–3.
21 Gentles, 'Arrears of Pay and Ideology', 51.
22 Woolrych, *Soldiers*, 151.
23 Woodhouse, 401–3; Woolrych, *Soldiers*, 116–17.
24 Kenyon, 263–8.
25 Ibid., 264; Woolrych, *Soldiers*, 117–18.
26 Gardiner, *GCW*, iii.318, 340 (quoted).
27 Ibid., iii.341.
28 Gentles, *New Model*, 181.
29 Woolrych, *Soldiers*, 168–72; Lindley, 142–3.
30 Gentles, *New Model*, 190–4.
31 Gardiner, *GCW*, iii.351–2.
32 Gentles, *New Model*, 199–200.
33 Kenyon, 274–6.
34 This point, and some of what follows, is based on a seminar paper by Phil Baker and Elliot Vernon on the Agreement of the People, given at the Institute of Historical Research, London, in June 2007.
35 A. Woolrych, 'The Debates from the Perspective of the Army', in Mendle, 68, 70–1.
36 Woodhouse, 53.
37 I. Gentles, 'The Agreements of the People and their Political Contexts', in Mendle, 153; Woolrych, *Soldiers*, 246–7; Gentles, *New Model*, 214–15, 217.
38 Woolrych, *Soldiers*, 262–5; Gentles, *New Model*, 218–19.
39 A. Thomson, *The Ware Mutiny of 1647* (Ware, 1996), 33–8; Gentles, *New Model*, 221–2.
40 Thomson, *Ware Mutiny*, 59–61, 88, 93–8 (quotation from p. 59); Gentles, *New Model*, 223–4; Woolrych, *Soldiers*, 286–9; Gentles, 'Agreements', in Mendle, 155.
41 Gentles, *New Model*, 227–34.

Chapter 8
1 Gardiner, *Documents*, 347–52.
2 Woolrych, *Soldiers*, 321.
3 Ashton, *Counter-Revolution*, 360–1.
4 I. Gentles, 'The Struggle for London in the Second Civil War', *HJ*, 26 (1983), 287–9.

5   Ashton, *Counter-Revolution*, 369–73.
6   Ibid., 152.
7   Lindley, 164–6.
8   Underdown, *Pride's Purge*, 99.
9   Carlton, *Going to the Wars*, 321–3. See also Gentles, *New Model*, 250–7.
10 P. Crawford, 'Charles Stuart, that Man of Blood', *Journal of British Studies*, 16/2 (1977), 41–61, especially p. 54.
11 J. Morrill and P. Baker, 'Oliver Cromwell, the Regicide and the Sons of Zeruiah', in Peacey, 26.
12 Gardiner, *GCW*, iv.168–9.
13 Gentles, *New Model*, 298.
14 Gardiner, *GCW*, iv.210.
15 Underdown, *Pride's Purge*, 59.
16 Gardiner, *GCW*, iv.220–1, 223.
17 S. Kelsey, 'The Death of Charles I', *HJ*, 45 (2002), 729–31.
18 W. Haller and G. Davies (eds), *The Leveller Tracts, 1647–53* (New York, 1944), 148–55.
19 Gentles, *New Model*, 267–70.
20 Gardiner, *GCW*, iv.238, 241–3.
21 Gentles, *New Model*, 274–6.
22 Underdown, *Pride's Purge*, 147–52.
23 Gentles, *New Model*, 286–7, 292–3.
24 See Kelsey, 'The Death of Charles I', *passim*.
25 Morrill and Baker, 'Sons of Zeruiah', in Peacey, 30.
26 Gardiner, *GCW*, iv.286.
27 Ibid., iv.290–1.
28 Ibid., iv.299.
29 Ibid., iv.301.
30 Ibid., iv.308, 313.
31 Carlton, *Charles I*, 252.
32 Gardiner, *GCW*, iv.322.

Epilogue

1   Gardiner, *GCW*, iv.294.
2   Underdown, *Pride's Purge*, 339.
3   A. Keay, *The Magnificent Monarch*, (Continuum, 2008).

BIBLIOGRAPHY

Adamson, J., *The Noble Revolt: The Overthrow of Charles I*, London, 2007.

Ashton, R., *Counter-Revolution: The Second Civil War and its Origins, 1646–8*, New Haven, 1994.

Canny, N., *Making Ireland British, 1580–1650*, Oxford, 2001.

Carlton, C., *Charles I: The Personal Monarch*, London, 1983.

———, *Going to the Wars: The Experience of the British Civil Wars, 1638–51*, London, 1992.

Cressy, D., *England on Edge: Crisis and Revolution 1640–2*, Oxford, 2006.

Everitt, A., *The Community of Kent and the Great Rebellion 1640–60*, Leicester, 1966.

Fletcher, A., *The Outbreak of the English Civil War*, London, 1981.

Gentles, I., *The New Model Army in England, Scotland and Ireland, 1645–53*, Oxford, 1992.

Holmes, C., *The Eastern Association in the English Civil War*, Cambridge, 1974.

Hughes, A., *Politics, Society and Civil War in Warwickshire, 1620–60*, Cambridge, 1987.

Hutton, R., *The Royalist War Effort 1642–6*, London, 1982.

Kishlansky, M., *The Rise of the New Model Army*, Cambridge, 1979.

Moody, T.W., F.X. Martin and F.J. Byrne (eds), *A New History of Ireland*. Vol. 3: *Early Modern Ireland, 1534–1691*, Oxford, 1976.

Morrill, J., *Cheshire, 1630–60*, Oxford, 1974.

——, *The Nature of the English Revolution*, London, 1993.

——, (ed.), *The Impact of the English Civil War*, London, 1991.

Pearl, V., *London and the Outbreak of the Puritan Revolution*, Oxford, 1961.

——, 'London's Counter-Revolution', in G.E. Aylmer (ed.), *The Interregnum*, London, 1972.

Richardson, R.C. (ed.), *The English Civil Wars: Local Aspects*, Stroud, 1997.

Russell, C., *The Causes of the English Civil War*, Oxford, 1990.

——, *The Fall of the British Monarchies, 1637–42*, Oxford, 1991.

Scott, D., *Politics and War in the Three Stuart Kingdoms, 1637–49*, Basingstoke, 2004.

Stoyle, M., *Loyalty and Locality: Popular Allegiance in Devon in the English Civil War*, Exeter, 1994.

Underdown, D., *Pride's Purge: Politics in the English Revolution*, Oxford, 1971.

——, *Revel Riot and Rebellion: Popular Politics and Culture in England, 1603–60*, Oxford, 1985.

Walter, J., *Understanding Popular Violence in the English Revolution: The Colchester Plunderers*, Cambridge, 1999.

Woolrych, A., *Soldiers and Statesmen: The General Council of the Army, 1647–8*, Oxford, 1987.

INDEX